Madrid &

Central Spain

Mary-Ann Gallagher

D1101655

Credits

Footprint credits

Editor: Nicola Gibbs
Maps: Kevin Feeney
Cover: Pepi Bluck

Publisher: Patrick Dawson
Advertising: Elizabeth Taylor
Sales and marketing: Kirsty Holmes

Photography credits

Front cover: LianeM/Shutterstock.com
Back cover: Matej Kastelic/Shutterstock.com

Printed in Great Britain by CPI Antony Rowe,
Chippenham, Wiltshire

Every effort has been made to ensure that
the facts in this guidebook are accurate.
However, travellers should still obtain advice
from consulates, airlines etc about travel
and visa requirements before travelling.
The authors and publishers cannot accept
responsibility for any loss, injury or
inconvenience however caused.

Publishing information

Footprint *Focus Madrid and Central Spain*
1st edition
© Footprint Handbooks Ltd
February 2013

ISBN: 978 1 909268 01 2
CIP DATA: A catalogue record for this book
is available from the British Library

Published by Footprint
6 Riverside Court,
Lower Bristol Road, Bath BA2 3DZ, UK
T +44 (0)1225 469141
F +44 (0)1225 469461
www.footprinttravelguides.com

The content of Footprint *Focus Madrid and
Central Spain* has been taken directly from
Footprint's *Spain Handbook*, which was
researched and written by Mary-Ann
Gallagher and Andy Symington.

Contents

5   Introduction
   4   *Map: Madrid and Central Spain*

4   Planning your trip
   6   Best time to visit Madrid and Central Spain
   6   Getting to Madrid and Central Spain
   8   Transport in Madrid and Central Spain
   10 Where to stay in Madrid and Central Spain
   12 Food and drink in Madrid and Central Spain
   19 Festivals in Madrid and Central Spain
   21 Essentials A-Z

25 Madrid and Central Spain
   26 Madrid
   28 *Map: Madrid*
   32 *Map: Madrid centre*
   58 Listings
   74 Central Spain
   78 *Map: Segovia*
   84 *Map: Ávila*
   92 *Map: Toledo*
   98 Listings

107 Background
   108 Architecture
   115 Art

121 Footnotes
   122 Useful words and phrases
   125 Food glossary
   126 Index

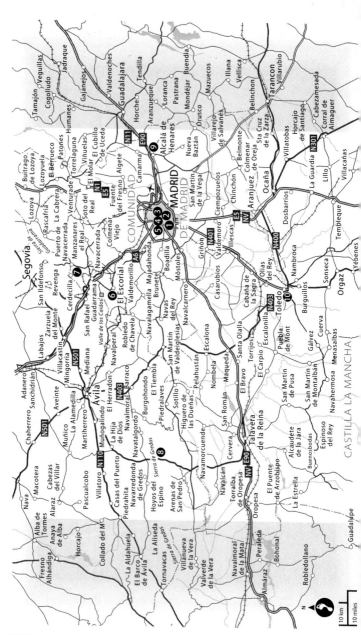

Madrid is not a city of half-measures: Europe's highest, greenest, youngest, sunniest capital likes to boast Desde Madrid al Cielo ('from Madrid to Heaven') with its matter-of-fact assumption that when you've seen Madrid, the only place left is Heaven. Perversely, the city is almost as famous for what it lacks as for what it boasts – there's no great river, no architectural marvels, no immediate picture-postcard charm. But what it does have, it has in spades: a fabulous collection of Western art held in the great triumvirate of the Prado, the Thyssen and the Reina Sofía, and an intense nightlife that makes most other cities look staid and past it.

The streets where Cervantes and Lope de Vega bickered and which later provided Goya with a backdrop for his paintings of local fiestas are still the heart of the city and remain delightfully walkable. A deliberately aimless stroll will throw up an outrageously lavish doorway, a Moorish flourish on a former belltower, or a boho-chic café set in an old pharmacy advertising laxatives in 19th-century tiles. The Spanish gift for combining tradition and modernity with such effortless aplomb reaches new heights in Madrid, a city in which miracles can still happen in one part of the city while a glossy new nightclub is being toasted in another.

And within just an hour or so drive of the capital, you can take your pick of lavish Bourbon palaces, monolithic monasteries, remote mountain villages and ancient cities. The mountains of the Sierra de Guadarrama are visible even from Madrid, and tucked away in their depths is Felipe II's massive palace-monastery of El Escorial and Franco's bombastic memorial to the fallen of the Civil War. The mountains also provide the backdrop for one of the most alluring cities in the area, Segovia, built of golden stone and crowned with a fairytale castle.

Planning your trip

Best time to visit Madrid and Central Spain

The vast Castilian plain with the capital Madrid at the centre famously bakes in summer and freezes in winter, so late spring and early autumn are the best times to visit to avoid the extremes of temperature. In winter you can even go skiing in the Sierra de Guadarrama.

Spain has a packed calendar of festivals, see page 19, which take place throughout the year, and there is almost always something going on in even the smallest village. Some of the biggest in Madrid and around include San Isidro in mid-May, and the neighbourhood festivals held in July and August. You'll have to book accommodation months in advance for any of these. See also Public holidays, page 20.

Getting to Madrid and Central Spain

Air

Madrid is one of Europe's most popular holiday destinations and there are hundreds of flights run by dozens of operators. This usually means a good deal for visitors, but you have to be prepared to shop around. Fares depend on the season and the kind of ticket you buy. Ticket prices are lowest in February, November and August. One of the best ways of finding the cheapest offers is to look on the internet; check out flight comparison sites such as www.skyscanner.net, www.momondo.com or www.fly.com. Companies such as www.ebookers.co.uk, www.expedia.co.uk and www.lastminute.com regularly offer good deals which are worth looking out for.

Students and those under 26 could consider booking through a specialist travel agent such as STA, www.statravel.co.uk, which has offices worldwide, or Trailfinders, www.trailfinders.com, in the UK, or Council Travel in the USA.

Airport information

Madrid Barajas Airport (MAD) is located about 13 km north of the city centre. It is Spain's main airport and one of the busiest in Europe. There are four terminals which offer both national and international flights from more than 40 airlines. There are tourist information offices in Terminals 1, 2 and 3, and all have ATMs, cafés and shops. Getting into the city is easy. You can take the metro (line 8) which has stations at Terminal 2 (for Terminals 1, 2 and 3) and at Terminal 4 (metro tickets to/from the airport cost €5), or catch the express bus service (€5, about 40 minutes to Atocha in the city centre). There's also a local bus service, which is cheaper (€1.50) but takes considerably longer. A taxi into the city centre will cost around €30.

Rail

Travelling from the UK to Spain by train is unlikely to save either time or money; the only two advantages lie in the pleasure of the journey itself and the chance to stop along the way. You can take the Eurostar (www.eurostar.com, T08342-186186) to Paris, the main rail gateway from the rest of Europe to Spain, which has overnight sleeper-train services to Madrid. The AVE high-speed rail network has been expanded in recent years; currently

Don't miss...

1   El Triángulo de Arte, page 40.
2   El Rastro flea market, page 50.
3   Shopping in the districts of Chueca, page 52, or Salamanca, page 55.
4   Parque del Retiro, page 46.
5   Tapas bar crawl in La Latina, page 62.
6   El Escorial, page 75.
7   Cotos, page 76.
8   Sierra de Gredos, page 86.
9   Alcalá de Henares, page 88.
10 Toledo, page 91.

the train from Paris to Madrid takes about 9½ hours (including a change in Figueras) but is expected to drop to seven hours eventually. For more information, contact www.sncf.fr (also in English), or www.raileurope.co.uk (in the UK) or www.raileurope.com (in North America). Fares vary considerably; the overnight train to Madrid costs from €400 for a return (AVE €400-600 return), but you'll need to book these fares in advance.

Road
Car The main routes into Spain are the E05/E70 motorway that runs down the southwest coast of France, crossing into Spain at Irun, near San Sebastián, and the E7, which crosses the eastern Pyrenees to Barcelona. Both these motorways are fairly heavily tolled but worthwhile compared to the slow, traffic-plagued *rutas nacionales* on these sectors. Several more scenic but much slower routes cross the Pyrenees at various points. Motorways charge expensive tolls in France and Spain and ferry fares can be extremely expensive in high season. Petrol is considerably more expensive than in North America but slightly cheaper in Spain than in France or the UK. For information on driving through France and traffic information, visit www.autoroute.fr.

Coach There are no direct bus services from the UK to Spain, you will need to change in Paris and buy separate tickets for each leg of the journey. Book well in advance and the entire journey could cost less than €50 (€100 return), but you will usually find a cheaper air fare and journey times can be long (between 24 and 36 hours). Eurolines ① *52 Grosvenor Gardens, London SW1, T08717-818178*, runs buses from major European cities to a variety of destinations in Spain, including Madrid.

Sea
Brittany Ferries ① *T08705-360360, www.brittanyferries.co.uk, office at the Estación Marítima, Santander, T942 360 611*, offers a ferry service from Plymouth to Santander, 100 west of Bilbao. These leave the UK up to five times a week, taking around 20 hours. Prices are variable but can usually be had for about £300 for a car and two passengers. They also offer a Portsmouth–Bilbao service, which operates twice a week and takes 24-32 hours. Fares are also around £300-500 for a car and two passengers, depending on the season.

Transport in Madrid and Central Spain

Public transport is generally good in Spain. You can expect several buses a day between adjacent provincial capitals; these services are quick, efficient, and nearly always beat the train over a given route. Once off the main routes, however, it's a different story. Don't expect to get to those picturesque rural monasteries if you're not prepared to hitch, walk, or hire a car. There are high-speed train links to many destinations around Madrid, including Toledo.

Rail

The Spanish national rail network RENFE ⓘ T902 320 320, www.renfe.com, offers a wide variety of services. The website (also in English) has online timetables and ticketing. You will probably use the local train service (**Cercanías**) most, either for getting around the city or reaching destinations further afield, such as El Escorial. Express services will take you to Toledo.

Road

Bus Buses are the staple of Spanish public transport. Services are usually fast, frequent, reliable, and fairly cheap. When booking, check whether you are getting a local or an express service (there's usually a supplement for express services). Most tickets will have a seat number (*asiento*) on them; ask when buying the ticket if you prefer a window (*de ventana*) or aisle (*de pasillo*) seat. If you're travelling at busy times (particularly a fiesta or national holiday) always book the bus ticket ahead. All bus services are reduced on Sundays, and many on Saturdays too; some services don't run at all on weekends.

Rural bus services are slower, less frequent, and more difficult to co-ordinate. They typically run early in the morning and late in the evening; they're designed for villagers who visit the 'big smoke' once a month or so to shop. If you're trying to catch a bus from a small stop, you'll often need to almost jump out under the wheels to get the driver to pull up. The same goes when trying to get off a bus; even if you've asked the driver to let you know when your stop comes up, keep an eye out as they tend to forget. There are hundreds of different bus companies but most bus stations have an information window and a general inquiry line to help you out. Unfortunately, English is rarely spoken, even in the larger towns. The tourist information offices usually have timetables for bus services to tourist destinations and are a good first port-of-call before you brave the ranks of ticket windows.

While most large villages will have at least some bus service to their provincial capital, the same doesn't apply for many touristed spots; it's assumed that all tourists have cars.

Most Spanish cities have their sights closely packed into the centre, so you won't find local buses particularly necessary. There's a fairly comprehensive network in most towns, though; the travel text throughout the book indicates where they come in handy.

Car The roads in Spain are good, excellent in many parts. While driving isn't as sedate as in parts of northern Europe, it's generally pretty good, and you'll have few problems. To drive in Spain, you'll need a full driving licence from your home country. This applies to virtually all foreign nationals, but, in practice, if you're from an 'unusual' country, consider an International Driving Licence or official translation of your licence into Spanish. Drivers are required by law to wear seatbelts, and to carry warning triangles, spares (tyres, bulbs, fanbelt) and the tools to fit them. You may also need to fit special prisms to your headlights for driving on the right if you are bringing your car from the UK or Ireland (so that they dip to the right). Front and rear seatbelts are compulsory, and children under 12 years are not permitted to ride in the front seat. Traffic circulates on the right.

There are two types of motorway in Spain: *autovías* and *autopistas*. A toll is required for *autopistas*, but otherwise they are virtually the same. Tolls are expensive, but the roads are normally good quality. The speed limit on motorways is 120 kph.

Rutas Nacionales form the backbone of Spain's road network. Centrally administered, they vary wildly in quality. Typically, they are choked with traffic backed up behind trucks, and there are few stretches of dual carriageway. Driving at siesta time is a good idea if you're going to be on a busy stretch. *Rutas Nacionales* are marked with a red N number. The speed limit is 100 kph outside built-up areas, as it is for secondary roads, which are numbered with the prefix 'C'.

In urban areas, the **speed limit** is 50 kph. Many towns and villages have sensors that will turn traffic lights red if you're over the limit on approach. City driving can be confusing, with signposting generally poor and traffic heavy. While not overly concerned about rural speed limits, police enforce the urban limits quite thoroughly; foreign drivers are liable to a large on-the-spot fine. Drivers can also be punished for not carrying two red warning triangles to place on the road in case of breakdown.

Parking is a problem, particularly in Madrid and the bigger cities. Red or yellow lines on the side of the street mean no parking. Blue or white lines mean that some restrictions are in place; a sign will indicate what these are (typically it means that the parking is metered). Parking meters can usually only be dosed up for a maximum of two hours, but they take a siesta at lunchtime too. Print the ticket off and display it in the car. Underground parking stations are common but fairly pricey: €20-30 a day is normal in the centre of Madrid, less in smaller cities.

Liability **insurance** is required for every car driven in Spain and you must carry proof of it. If bringing your own car, check carefully with your insurers that you're covered, and get a certificate (green card). If your insurer doesn't cover you for breakdowns, consider joining the **RACE** ① *T902 404 545, www.race.es*, Spain's automobile association, which provides breakdown cover.

Car hire in Spain is easy but not especially cheap. The major multinationals have offices at all large towns and airports; cheaper organizations include **ATESA**, www.atesa.es, which has offices at most of the larger train stations, and **Holiday Autos**, www.holidayautos.com. All major international car hire firms including **Avis**, www.avis.com; **National**, www.nationalcar.com (who often share offices with ATESA); **Hertz**, www.hertz.com are all represented in most cities. It's also worth checking with your airline when you book your flight if they offer any special deals on car rental. Prices start at around €150 per week for a small car with unlimited mileage. You'll need a credit card and your passport, and most agencies will either not accept under-25s or demand a surcharge.

Cycling Cycling presents a curious contrast; Spaniards are mad for the competitive sport, but comparatively uninterested in cycling as a means of transport. Thus there are plenty of cycling shops (although beware, it can be time-consuming to find replacement parts for non-standard cycles) but very few bike lanes. Madrid, despite improvements in recent years, remains one of the worst cities in Spain to cycle. It's best to escape to the surrounding mountains if you want to enjoy your bike ride. Contact the **Real Federación Española de Ciclismo**, www.rfec.com, for more links and assistance.

Motorcycling Motorcycling is a good way to enjoy Spain, and there are few difficulties to trouble the biker; bike shops and mechanics are relatively common. Hiring a motorbike, however, can be difficult; most outlets are in the major cities. **Real Federación Motociclista Española** can help with links and advice; their website is www.rfme.com.

Taxis Taxis are a convenient and reasonable option; flagfall is €2.15 in Madrid plus €1 per kilometre . A taxi is available if its green light is lit; hail one on the street or ask for the nearest rank (*parada de taxis*).

Maps
The Michelin series of road maps are by far the most accurate for general navigation, although if you're getting off the beaten track you'll often find a local map handy. Tourist offices provide these, which vary in quality from province to province. The *Everest* series of maps cover provinces and their main towns; they're not bad, although tend to be a bit out of date. The **Instituto Geográfico Nacional** publishes provincial maps, available at bookshops. Good bookshops in Madrid include **Altair** ① *C/Gaztambide 31, T915 455 300, www.altair.es*. Pick up maps in advance from **Stanford's** ① *12 Long Acre, London, WC2, T020-7836 1321, www.stanfords.co.uk*. In the USA, **The Traveler's Choice Bookstore** ① *2 Wooster St, New York, T(212)941 1535*, has a good selection.

Where to stay in Madrid and Central Spain

The standard of accommodation in Spain is reasonably high: even the most modest of *pensiones* are usually very clean and respectable. However, a great number of Spanish hotels are well-equipped but characterless places on the ugly edges of town. This guide has expressly minimized these in the listings, preferring to concentrate on more atmospheric options. If booking accommodation using this guide, always be sure to check the location if that's important to you – it's easy to find yourself a 15-minute cab ride from the town you want to be in.

All registered accommodations charge a 10% value-added tax (IVA); this is often included at cheaper places and may be waived if you pay cash. If you have any problems, a last resort is to ask for the *libro de reclamaciones* (complaints book), an official document that, like stepping on cracks in the pavement, means uncertain but definitely horrible consequences for the hotel if anything is written in it.

Hoteles, hostales and pensiones
Places to stay (*alojamientos*) are divided into three main categories; the distinctions between them are in an arcane series of regulations devised by the government. *Hoteles* (marked H or HR) are graded from one to five stars and usually occupy their own building, which distinguishes them from *hostales* (Hs or HsR), which go from one to three stars. *Pensiones* (P) are the standard budget option, and are usually family-run flats in an apartment block. Although it's worth looking at a room before taking it, the majority are

Price codes

Where to stay

€€€€ over €170   **€€€**   €110-170

€€   €55-110   **€**   under €55

Prices include taxes and service charge, but not meals. They are based on a double room, except in the **€** range, where prices are almost always per person.

Restaurants

€€€ over €20   **€€** €10-20   **€** under €10

Prices refer to the cost of a two-course meal, without a drink.

very acceptable. The Spanish traditions of hospitality are alive and well; even the simplest of *pensiones* will generally provide a towel and soap, and check-out time is almost uniformly a very civilized midday.

Paradors

Spain's famous chain of state-owned hotels, the paradors, are often set in castles, convents and other historic buildings, although there are plenty of modern ones too. Most are very luxurious, with pools, bars, fine restaurants and other fancy trimmings but standards can vary considerably. They are usually expensive, but they offer all kinds of special deals, including a youth package, which can make them surprisingly affordable. Contact one of their representatives in your own country (addresses below) or check out the website: www.parador.es. There are eight paradors in the region around Madrid: the ones in Alcalá de Henares and La Granja are two of the chain's newest, both set in superb historic buildings.

Rural homes

An excellent option if you've got transport are the networks of rural homes, called a variety of things from *agroturismos* to *casas rurales*. Although these are under a different classification system, the standard is often as high as any country hotel. The best of them are traditional farmhouses or old village cottages. Some are available to rent out whole, while others operate more or less as hotels. Rates tend to be excellent compared to hotels. Each regional government publishes their own listings booklet, which is available at any tourist office in the area or you could check out the websites such as www.toprural.com.

Albergues and refugios

There are a few youth hostels (*albergues*) around, but the price of *pensiones* rarely makes it worth the trouble except for solo travellers. Spanish youth hostels are frequently populated by schoolkids and have curfews and check-out times unsuitable for the late hours the locals keep. The exception is in mountain regions, where there are *refugios*; basically simple hostels for walkers and climbers along the lines of a Scottish bothy. Some official youth hostels require an international youth hostel card, available in advance from the international Youth Hostel Associations.

Campsites

Most campsites are set up as well-equipped holiday villages for families; many are open only in summer. While the facilities are good, they get extremely busy in peak season; the social scene is good, but sleep can be tough. In other areas, camping, unless specifically prohibited, is a matter of common sense: most locals will know of (or offer) a place where you can pitch a tent *tranquilamente*.

Food and drink in Madrid and Central Spain

Madrileños eat very little for breakfast, usually just a coffee and maybe a croissant or pastry. They might tuck into *chocolate y churros* – thick, sticky hot chocolate with thin donut-like batter strips. They may have a quick bite and a drink in a café or bar before lunch, which is usually eaten between 1400-1530 or thereabouts. This is the main meal of the day and the cheapest time to eat, as most restaurants offer a cheap set menu (*menú del día*). Lunch (and dinner) is much extended at weekends, particularly on Sundays, when it seems to go on until the football kicks off in the evening. It's common to have an evening drink or *tapa* in a bar after the *paseo*, if this is extended into a food crawl it's called a *tapeo*. Dinner (*cena*) is normally eaten from about 2200 onwards, although sitting down to dinner at midnight at weekends isn't unusual. In smaller towns and midweek you might not get fed after 2230, so beware. Most restaurants are closed Sunday nights, and usually take a day off, either Monday or Tuesday.

Food → *See box, page 11, for price code information, and the Food glossary, page 125.*

While the regional differences in the cuisine of Spain are important, the basics remain the same. Spanish cooking relies on meat, fish/seafood, beans and potatoes given character by the chef's holy trinity: garlic, peppers and, of course, olive oil. The influence of the colonization of the Americas is evident, and the Moors left a lasting culinary legacy, particularly in the south. The result is a hearty, filling style of meal ideally washed down with some of the nation's excellent wines. In Madrid, as befits a nation's capital, you can eat your way around the entire country, with restaurants dedicated to the cuisine of every region.

Fish and seafood   Despite being inland, there is always good availability of fresh fish and seafood in Madrid. *Merluza* (hake) and *bacalao* (salt cod) are the staple fish, while *gambas* (prawns) are another common and excellent choice. Calamari, squid and cuttlefish are common; if you can cope with the slightly slimy texture, *pulpo* (octopus) is particularly good, especially when simply boiled *a la gallega* (Galician style) and flavoured with paprika and olive oil. Supreme among the finny tribe are *rodaballo* (turbot, best wild or *salvaje*) and *rape* (monkfish). Fresh trout from the mountain streams of Northern Spain are hard to beat too; they are commonly cooked with bacon or ham (*trucha a la navarra*).

Meat   Wherever you go, you'll find cured ham (*jamón serrano*), which is always excellent, but particularly so if it's the pricey *ibérico*, taken from acorn-eating porkers in Extremadura. Other cold meats to look out for are *cecina*, made from beef, and, of course, sausages (*embutidos*), including the versatile *chorizo*.

Pork is also popular as a cooked meat; its most common form is sliced loin (*lomo*). The Castilian plains specialize in roast sucking pig (*cochinillo* or *lechón*), usually a sizeable dish indeed. *Lechazo* is the lamb equivalent, popular in mountainous regions. Beef is common throughout; cheaper cuts predominate, but the better steaks (*solomillo*, *chuletón*) are usually superbly tender. Spaniards tend to eat them rare (*poco hecho*; ask for *a punto* for medium or *bien hecho* for well-done). The *chuletón* is worth a mention in its own right; a massive T-bone best taken from an ox (*de buey*) and sold by weight, which often approaches a kilogram. It's an imposing slab of meat indeed. *Pollo* (chicken) is common, but usually unremarkable; game birds such as *codorniz* (quail) and *perdiz* (partridge) are also widely eaten. The innards of animals are very popular in Madrid; *callos* (tripe), *mollejas* (sweetbreads), and *morcilla* (black pudding in solid or liquid form) are all excellent, if acquired, tastes. Fans of the unusual will be keen to try *jabalí* (wild boar), *potro* (horse) and *oreja* (ear, usually from a pig or sheep).

Vegetable dishes and accompaniments Main dishes often come without any accompaniments, or chips at best. The consolation, however, is the *ensalada mixta*, whose simple name (mixed salad) can often conceal a meal in itself. The ingredients vary, but it's typically a plentiful combination of lettuce, tomato, onion, olive oil, boiled eggs, asparagus, olives and tuna. The tortilla, see box, page 15, is ever-present and often excellent. Another common dish is *revuelto* (scrambled eggs), usually tastily combined with prawns, asparagus or other goodies.

Most vegetable dishes are based around that American trio, the bean, the pepper, and the potato. There are numerous varieties of beans in Spain; they are normally served as some sort of hearty stew, often with bits of meat or seafood to avoid the accusation of vegetarianism. *Fabada* is the Asturian classic of this variety, while *alubias con chorizo* are a standard across the northern Spain. The Catalan version is *faves a la catalana*, broad beans cooked with ham. A *cocido* is a typical mountain dish from the centre of Spain, a massive stew of chickpeas or beans with meat and vegetables. Peppers (*pimientos*), too, come in a confusing number of forms. As well as being used to flavour dishes, they are often eaten in their own right; *pimientos rellenos* come stuffed with meat or seafood. Potatoes come as chips, *bravas* (with a garlic or spicy tomato sauce) or, more interestingly, *a la riojana*, with chorizo and paprika. Other common vegetable dishes include *menestra* (think of a good minestrone soup with the liquid drained off), which usually has some ham in it, and *ensaladilla rusa*, a tasty blend of potato, peas, peppers, carrots and mayonnaise. *Setas* (wild mushrooms) are a particular delight, especially in autumn, but they are rarely found in the south. See page 19 for the lowdown on eating out as a vegetarian.

Desserts and cheeses Desserts focus on the sweet and milky. *Flan* (a sort of crème caramel) is ubiquitous; great when *casero* (home-made), but often out of a plastic tub. *Natillas* are a similar but more liquid version, and *arroz con leche* is a cold, sweet rice pudding.

Cheeses tend to be bland or salty and are normally eaten as a *tapa* or entrée. There are some excellent cheeses in Spain, however; the most famous is the dry, pungent Manchego, a cured sheep's milk cheese from La Mancha, but piquant Cabrales and Basque Idiázabal also stand out.

Regional cuisine

Regional styles tend to use the same basic ingredients treated in slightly different ways, backed up by some local specialities. Food-producing regions take their responsibilities seriously, and competition is fierce. Those widely acknowledged to produce the best will often add the name of the region to the foodstuff (some foods, like wines, have denomination of origin status given by a regulatory body). Thus *pimientos de Padrón* (Padrón peppers), *cogollos de Tudela* (lettuce hearts from Tudela), *alubias de Tolosa* (Tolosa beans) and a host of others.

Typical **Madrileño** cuisine reflects the city's land-locked status in the middle of a vast plain; hunks of roast meats and hearty stews, like *cocido*, a thick broth of chickpeas, vegetables and hunks of meat, which are cooked together and served in separate courses – often over several days. Spaniards in general, and Madrileños in particular, don't turn their noses up at any part of an animal, and another local speciality is *callos a la madrileño*, a tripe dish cooked in a spicy tomato sauce. It's not unusual to find *orejas* (pigs' ears), *sesos* (brains), *riñones* (kidneys) and even *criadillas* (bulls' testicles) on the menu. If you head out to Segovia, be sure to try *cochinillo*, roast suckling pig, traditionally slaughtered when they are 21 days old. Ideally, it should be tender enough to cut with a butter knife.

Most of Spain grudgingly concedes that **Basque** cuisine is the peninsula's best, the San Sebastián twilight shimmers with Michelin stars, and chummy all-male *txokos* gather in private to swap recipes and cook up feasts in members-only kitchens. But what strikes the visitor first are the *pintxos*, a stunning range of bartop snacks that in many cases seem too pretty to eat. The base of most Basque dishes is seafood, particularly *bacalao* (salt cod; occasionally stunning but often humdrum), and the region has taken full advantage of its French ties.

Navarran and Aragonese cuisine owes much to the mountains, with hearty stews and game dishes featuring alongside fresh trout. **Rioja and Castilla y León** go for filling roast meat and bean dishes more suited to the harsh winters than the baking summers. **Asturias and Cantabria** are seafood-minded on the coast but search for more warming fare in the high ground, and Galicia is seafood heaven, with more varieties of finny and shelly things than you knew there were; usually prepared with confidence in the natural flavours, whereas the rest of the area overuses garlic to eliminate any fishy taste.

The **Catalans** are almost as famous for their cuisine as the Basques. Seafood from the Mediterranean, rice and vegetables from the plains and meat and game from the mountains are combined in unusual ways; look out for *mandonguilles amb sèpia*, meatballs with cuttlefish, or *gambas amb pollastre*, prawns with chicken. The local staple is *pa amb tomàquet*, country bread rubbed with fresh tomatoes, with a little olive oil and salt. **Valencia** is famous as the birthplace of *paella*, a surprisingly difficult dish that is often made badly elsewhere in Spain, much to the annoyance of Valencianos. The genuine article is made with starchy *bomba* rice grown in the Valencian plains, and real saffron (not yellow food colouring, which is common), which is simmered in a shallow pan with garlic and olive oil, and a mixture of meat and/or seafood (depending on the recipe – no one can agree on the ingredients of the definitive paella). The finishing touch is the *soccarat*, a crunchy crust formed by turning up the heat for a few minutes just before the paella is cooked.

A taste for tortilla

Tortilla is perhaps the classic dish of Spain. Served everywhere and eaten at virtually every time of the day, it is easy to prepare and can be eaten either hot or cold. Typically served as tapas or with a salad its key features are the layering of the potatoes and its rounded shape, enabling it to be eaten in slices.

Method (serves 6)
1 large frying pan for potatoes
1 small, fairly deep frying pan
6 fresh eggs
750 g of potatoes thinly sliced
half a medium onion (if desired)
enough good quality olive oil to cover the potatoes in a frying pan
salt
Total cooking and preparation time around 1 hour.

Wash and peel the potatoes then slice thinly so they are about ½ cm in thickness. Place them in a mixing bowl and sprinkle with salt ensuring that that each piece is coated with a little salt. Cut and slice the onion into small pieces about 2 cm long and add to the potatoes.

Place the salted potatoes and onions in a large frying pan and pour in enough olive oil nearly to cover the them. It is essential to use good quality oil – Spanish cooks would never dream of using inferior aceite

for tortilla. Keep the pan at a low heat and continue to stir the potatoes regularly to ensure they do not burn. The aim is to cook the potatoes while ensuring they do not become crisp. Remove the cooked potatoes and onion from the pan and drain the oil. Total cooking time should be between 15-20 minutes depending on the thickness of the potatoes.

Mix the eggs in a mixing bowl. It is not necessary to add salt as the potatoes should have enough seasoning. Milk and pepper are rarely used in Spanish cooking but will not radically affect the taste if preferred. Prepare a new smaller pan which is deep enough to contain the egg mix and the potatoes. Place the cooked and drained potatoes in first and then add the egg mix. Fry the mixture, keeping the heat very low. When the mixture is showing signs of becoming solid remove the pan from the heat and find a plate large enough to cover the pan.

The next stage is the only tricky bit as the mixture is now to be turned over to cook the other side. Turn the solid mix on to the plate and then return it to the pan ensuring the uncooked side is facing the bottom of the pan. Continue to cook until the tortilla is solid. Total frying time should be around 10 minutes. Remove the tortilla from the pan and eat either hot or leave to cool and eat later.

In **Andalucía**, the Moorish inheritance is felt most strongly. The Arabs cultivated olives, saffron and almonds, which all appear in the local cuisine. There's plenty of fresh seafood along the coast and *pescadito frito*, fried fresh fish best eaten out of a paper cone, is the specialitiy of Cádiz. Inland the emphasis is on meat and game: one of the region's best known dishes is *rabo de toro* – bull's tail slowly cooked in a rich sauce. You might already have tried *gazpacho* – a cold soup of tomatoes, onions and cucumber – but there's a delicious thicker version called *salmorejo*, usually topped with chopped ham and boiled eggs, and a white soup called *ajo blanco* in which the tomatoes have been replaced with almonds.

Extremadura is known for its *migas*, breadcrumbs fried with peppers, but it's most famous culinary export is the *jamón ibérico*. This is the king of hams – and Spain has countless varieties – and is made from the flesh of the *pata negra* (black foot) pigs which roam the Extremaduran *dehesa* and are fed on acorns. Watch out, though, if you order it in a tapas bar; it's very, very expensive.

Drink

Wine In good Catholic fashion, wine is the blood of Spain. It's the standard accompaniment to most meals, but also features prominently in bars, where a glass of cheap *tinto* or *blanco* can cost as little as €1, although it's normally more. A bottle of house wine in a restaurant is often no more than €8 or €9. *Tinto* is red (although if you just order *vino* it's assumed that's what you want), *blanco* is white, and rosé is either *clarete* or *rosado*.

A well-regulated system of *denominaciones de origen* (DO), similar to the French *appelation controlée*, has lifted the reputation of Spanish wines high above the party plonk status they once enjoyed. Much of Spain's wine is produced in the north, and recent years have seen regions such as the Ribera del Duero, Rueda, Navarra, Pinedes and Rías Baixas achieve worldwide recognition. But the daddy is, of course, still Rioja.

The overall standard of Riojas has improved markedly since the granting of the higher DOC status in 1991, with some fairly stringent testing in place. Red predominates; these are mostly medium-bodied bottles from the Tempranillo grape (with three other permitted red grapes often used to add depth or character). Whites from Viura and Malvasia are also produced: the majority of these are young, fresh and dry, unlike the powerful oaky Rioja whites sold in the UK. Rosés are also produced. The quality of individual Riojas varies widely according to both producer and the amount of time the wines have been aged in oak barrels and in the bottle. The words *crianza*, *reserva*, and *gran reserva* refer to the length of the aging process (see below), while the vintage date is also given. Rioja producers store their wines at the *bodega* until deemed ready for drinking, so it's common to see wines dating back a decade or more on shelves and wine lists.

A growing number of people feel, however, that Spain's best reds come from further west, in the Ribera del Duero region east of Valladolid. The king's favourite tipple, *Vega Sicilia*, has long been Spain's most prestigious wine, but other producers from the area have also gained stellar reviews. The region has been dubbed 'the Spanish Burgundy'; the description isn't wholly fanciful, as the better wines have the rich nose and dark delicacy vaguely reminiscent of the French region.

Galicia produces some excellent whites too; the coastal Albariño vineyards produce a sought-after dry wine with a very distinctive bouquet. Ribeiro is another good Galician white, and the reds from there are also tasty, having some similarity to those produced in nearby northern Portugal.

Among other regions, Navarra, long known only for rosé, is producing some quality red wines unfettered by the stricter rules governing production in neighbouring Rioja, while Bierzo, in western León province, also produces interesting wines from the red Prieto Picudo grape. Other DO wines in Northern Spain include Somontano, a red and white appellation from Aragón and Toro, whose baking climate makes for full-bodied reds.

An unusual wine worth trying is *txakolí*, with a small production on the Basque coast. The most common form is a young, refreshing, acidic white which has a green tinge and a slight sparkle, often accentuated by pouring from a height. The best examples, from around Getaria, go beautifully with seafood. The wine is made from underripe grapes of the Ondarrubi Zuria variety; there's a less common red species and some rosé.

Catalan wines are also gaining increasing recognition. Best known is *cava*, the home-grown bubbly, and a night out in Barcelona should always start with a glass or two of this crisp, sparkling white wine. The largest wine-producing region in Catalunya is Penedès, which produces a vast range of reds, whites and rosés to suit all tastes and pockets, but you'll find other local specialities including the unusual *Paxarete*, a very sweet traditional chocolatey brown wine produced around Tarragona.

One of the joys of Spain, though, is the rest of the wine. Order a *menú del día* at a cheap restaurant and you'll be unceremoniously served a cheap bottle of local red (sometimes without even asking for it). Wine snobbery can leave by the back door at this point: it may be cold, but you'll find it refreshing; it may be acidic, but once the olive-oil laden food arrives, you'll be glad of it. Wine's not a luxury item in Spain, so people add water to it if they feel like it, or lemonade, or *cola* (to make the party drink called *calimocho*).

In many bars, you can order *Ribera*, *Rueda*, or other regions by the glass. If you simply ask for *crianza* or *reserva*, you'll usually get a Rioja. A *tinto* or *blanco* will get you the house wine (although many bartenders in tourist areas assume that visitors don't want it, and will try and serve you a more expensive kind). As a general rule, only bars that serve food serve wine; most *pubs* and *discotecas* won't have it.

Beer Spanish beer is mostly lager, usually reasonably strong, fairly gassy, cold, and good. On the tapas trail, many people order *cortos,* usually about 100 ml. A *caña* is a larger draught beer, usually about 200-300 ml. Order a *cerveza* and you'll get a bottled beer. Many people order their beer *con gas*, topped up with mineral water, sometimes called a *clara*, although this normally means it's topped with lemonade. A *jarra* is a shared jug.

Cider *Sidra* is an institution in Asturias, and to a lesser extent in Euskadi, but you'll find plenty of it in Madrid, Basque and Asturian restaurants. The cider is flat, sourish, and yeasty; the appley taste will be a surprise after most commercial versions of the drink. Typical Asturian *sidrerías* offer some of Spain's most enjoyable barlife with excellent food, a distinctive odour, sawdust on the floor, and the cider poured from above head height by uniformed waiters to give it some bounce.

Sherry If you thought sherry was for old ladies and vicars, think again. At Seville's famous *Feria*, the standard tipple is a glass of refreshing chilled *manzanilla*, a pale, dry and delicious thirst-quencher and it's almost as popular in Madrid's tapas bars in summer. There are dozens of other varieties including the light *fino* which is drunk young, or sweeter *amontillados* with a caramel flavour. The very sweetest are *olorosos*, a traditional dessert accompaniment.

Spirits Vermut (vermouth) is a popular pre-dinner *aperitif*, usually served straight from the barrel. Many bars make their own vermouth by adding various herbs and fruits and letting it sit in barrels: this can be excellent, particularly if its from a *solera*. This is a system where liquid is drawn from the oldest of a series of barrels, which is then topped up with the next oldest, etc, resulting in some very mellow characterful drink.

After dinner people relax over a whisky or a brandy, or hit the mixed drinks: *gin tonic* is obvious, while a *cuba libre* is a rum and coke (but can refer to vodka or other spirits). Spirits are free-poured and large; don't be surprised at a 100 ml measure. Whisky is popular, and most bars have a good range. Spanish brandy is good, although it's oaky vanilla flavours don't appeal to everyone. There are numerous varieties of rum and flavoured liqueurs. When ordering a spirit, you'll be expected to choose which brand you want; the local varieties (eg *Larios* gin, *DYC* whisky) are marginally cheaper than their imported brethren. *Chupitos* are shots; restaurants will often throw in a free one at the end of a meal, or give you a bottle of *orujo* (grape spirit) to pep up your black coffee.

Non-alcoholic drinks Juice is normally bottled and expensive, although freshly squeezed orange juice is common. It's an odd thing to order after breakfast, though. *Mosto* (grape juice; really pre-fermented wine) is a cheaper and popular soft drink in bars. There's the usual range of fizzy drinks (*gaseosas*) available, but a popular and peculiarly Spanish soft drink is *Bitter-kas*, a dark red herby brew which tastes a bit like Campari. *Horchata* is a summer drink, a sort of milkshake made from tiger nuts which comes from the Valencia region but is popular throughout Spain. Water (*agua*) comes *con* (with) or *sin* (without) *gas*. The tap water is totally safe to drink, but it's not always the nicest.

Hot drinks Coffee (*café*) is usually excellent and strong. *Solo* is black, mostly served espresso style. Order *americano* if you want a long black, *cortado* if you want a dash of milk, or *con leche* for about half milk. A *carajillo* is a coffee with brandy, while *queimado* is a coffee heated with *orujo*, a Galician drink of ritual significance. *Té* (tea) is served without milk unless you ask; herbal teas (*infusiones*) can be found in many places. *Chocolate* is a reasonably popular drink at breakfast time or as a *merienda* (afternoon tea), served with *churros*, fried doughsticks that seduce about a quarter of visitors and repel the rest.

Restaurants in Madrid and Central Spain
One of the great pleasures of travelling in Spain is eating out, but it's no fun sitting alone in a restaurant so try and adapt to the local hours as much as you can; it may feel strange leaving dinner until after 2200, but you'll miss out on a lot of atmosphere if you don't.

The standard distinctions of bar, café and restaurant don't apply in Spain. Many places combine all three functions, and it's not always evident; the dining room (*comedor*) is often tucked away behind the bar or upstairs. *Restaurantes* are restaurants, and will usually have a dedicated dining area with set menus and *à la carte* options. Bars and cafés will often display food on the counter, or have a list of tapas; bars tend to be known for particular dishes they do well. Many bars, cafés and restaurants don't serve food on Sunday nights, and most are closed one other night a week, most commonly Monday.

Cafés will normally have some breakfasty fare out in the mornings; croissants and sweetish pastries are the norm; fresh squeezed orange juice is also common. About 1100 they start putting out savoury fare; maybe a tortilla, some *ensaladilla rusa*, or little ham rolls in preparation for pre-lunch snacking.

Lunch is the biggest meal of the day for most people in Spain, and it's also the cheapest time to eat. Just about all restaurants offer a *menú del día*, which is usually a set three-course meal that includes wine or soft drink. In unglamorous workers' locals this is often as little as €7 or €8; paying anything more than €15 indicates the restaurant takes itself quite seriously. There's often a choice of several starters and mains. To make the most of the meal, a handy tip is to order another starter in place of a main; most places are quite happy to do it, and the starters are usually more interesting (and sometimes larger) than the mains, which tend to be slabs of mediocre meat. Most places open for lunch at about 1300, and stop serving at 1500 or 1530, although at weekends this can extend; it's not uncommon to see people still lunching at 1800 on a Sunday. The quality of *à la carte* is usually higher than the *menú*, and quantities are large. Simpler restaurants won't offer this option except in the evenings.

Tapas has changed in meaning over the years, and now basically refers to all bar food. Prices of tapas basically depend on the ingredients; a good portion of *langostinos* (king prawns) will likely set you back €12-15, while more *morcilla* (black pudding) or *patatas* than you can eat might only be €3 or so.

Most restaurants open for dinner at 2030 or later; any earlier and it's likely a tourist trap. Although some places do offer a cheap set menu, you'll usually have to order *à la carte*. In quiet areas, places stop serving at 2200 on weeknights, but in cities and at weekends people tend to sit down at 2230 or later.

A cheap option at any time of day is a *plato combinado*, most commonly done in cafés. They're usually a truckstop-style combination of eggs, steak, bacon and chips or similar and are filling but rarely inspiring.

Vegetarians in Spain won't be spoiled for choice, but at least what there is tends to be good. Dedicated vegetarian restaurants are amazingly few, and most restaurants won't have a vegetarian main course on offer, although the existence of *raciones* and salads makes this less of a burden than it might be. *Ensalada mixta* nearly always has tuna in it, but it's usually made fresh, so places will happily leave it out. *Ensaladilla rusa* is normally a good option, but ask about the tuna too, just in case. Tortilla is another simple but nearly ubiquitous option. Simple potato or pepper dishes are tasty options (although beware peppers stuffed with meat), and many *revueltos* (scrambled eggs) are just mixed with asparagus. Annoyingly, most vegetable *menestras* are seeded with ham before cooking, and bean dishes usually have at least some meat or animal fat. You'll have to specify *soy vegetariano/a* (I am a vegetarian), but ask what dishes contain, as ham, fish, and even chicken are often considered suitable vegetarian fare. Vegans will have a tougher time. What doesn't have meat nearly always has cheese or egg, and waiters are unlikely to know the ingredients down to the basics.

Festivals in Madrid and Central Spain

Even the smallest village in Central Spain has a fiesta, and some have several. Although mostly nominally religious in nature, they usually include the works; a mass and procession or two to be sure, but also live music, bullfights, competitions, fireworks and copious drinking of *calimocho*, a mix of red wine and cola (not as bad as it sounds). A feature of many are the *gigantes y cabezudos*, huge-headed papier-mâché figures based on historical personages who parade the streets. Adding to the sense of fun are peñas, boisterous social clubs which patrol the streets making music, get rowdy at the bullfights and drink wine all night and day. Most fiestas are in summer, and if you're spending much time in Spain in that period you're bound to run into one; expect some trouble finding accommodation. Details of the major town fiestas can be found in the travel text. National holidays can be difficult times to travel; it's important to reserve tickets in advance. If the holiday falls mid-week, it's usual form to take an extra day off, forming a long weekend known as a *puente* (bridge).

Major fiestas

5 January Cabalgata de Los Reyes (Three Kings). Throughout Spain. The Three Kings Parade in floats tossing out sweets to kids, who get Christmas presents the next day.

February/March Carnaval. Held in almost every town and village.

Easter Semana Santa. Easter celebrations are held everywhere and parades take place in every town.

8-15 May Fiestas de San Isidro. The second week of May is devoted to Madrid's patron saint, San Isidro, and has developed into a massive event, with live bands, parades and street parties all over Madrid. It also marks the opening of the bullfighting season, with several special bullfighting events.

End May/June Feast of Corpus Christi. Held in most towns, it is celebrated with traditional dancing and parades. Toledo's processions are the grandest.

21-24 June Fiesta de San Juan, or the Midsummer's Solstice. This is celebrated across Spain, often with bullfights, or with the strange custom of the 'Burial of the Sardine'.

Public holidays

1 January Año Nuevo (New Year's Day)

6 January Reyes Magos (Epiphany) when Christmas presents are given.

Easter Jueves Santo, Viernes Santo, Día de Pascua (Maundy Thursday, Good Friday, Easter Sunday).

1 May Fiesta de Trabajo (Labour Day).

15 August Asunción (Feast of the Assumption).

12 October Día de la Hispanidad (Columbus Day, Spanish National Day, Feast of the Virgin of the Pillar).

1 November Todos los Santos (All Saints' Day).

6 December El Día de la Constitución Española (Constitution Day).

8 December Inmaculada Concepción (Feast of the Immaculate Conception).

24 December Noche Buena (Christmas Eve).

25 December Navidad (Christmas Day).

Essentials A-Z

Accident and emergencies
There is now one nationwide emergency number for fire, police and ambulance: **T112**.

Electricity
The current in Spain is 220V. A round 2-pin plug is used (European standard).

Embassies and consulates
For embassies and consulates of Spain abroad, see http://embassy.goabroad.com.

Health → *See Directory, page 73, for hospitals and pharmacies in Madrid.*
Health for travellers in Spain is rarely a problem. Medical facilities are good, and the worst most travellers experience is an upset stomach, usually merely a result of the different diet rather than any bug. The water is safe to drink, but doesn't always taste great, so many travellers (and locals) stick to bottled water. The sun can be harsh, so take precautions to avoid heat exhaustion/ sunburn. Many medications that require a prescription in other countries are available over the counter at pharmacies in Spain. Pharmacists are highly trained but don't necessarily speak English. In all medium-sized towns and cities, at least one pharmacy is open 24 hrs; this is organized on a rota system; details are posted in the window of all pharmacies and listed in local newspapers.

Insurance
British and other European citizens should obtain a European Health Insurance Card (EHIC) available via www.dh.gov.uk or from post offices in the UK, before leaving home. This guarantees free medical care throughout the EU. Non-EU citizens should consider insurance to cover emergency and routine medical needs; be sure that it covers any sports/activities you may get involved in.

Insurance is a good idea anyway to cover you for theft, etc. Any theft must be reported at the local police station within 24 hrs; you'll need to obtain a written report to show your insurers. Visit **SATE** (Servicio de Atención al Turista Extranjero), which was set up to help foreign victims of crime, at the police station at C/Leganitos 19, Madrid, T902 102 112, metro Santo Domingo, open daily 0900-2400.

Language → *See page 126, for some useful words and phrases.*
For travelling purposes, everyone in Spain speaks Spanish, known either as *castellano* or *español*. Most young people know some English, and standards are rising, but don't assume that people aged 30 or over know any at all. While efforts to speak the language are appreciated, it's more or less expected, to the same degree as English is expected in Britain or the USA. Nobody will be rude if you don't speak any Spanish, but nobody will think to slow down their speech for your benefit either. While many visitor attractions have information available in English (and sometimes French and German), many don't, or only have English tours in times of high demand. Most tourist office staff will speak at least some English, and there's a good range of translated information available in many regions.

Money → *See www.xe.com for exchange rates.*
Currency
In 2002, Spain switched to the euro, bidding farewell to the peseta. The euro (€) is divided into 100 céntimos. Euro notes are standard across the whole zone, and come in denominations of 5, 10, 20, 50, 100, and the rarely seen 200 and 500. Coins have one standard face and one national face; all coins are, however, acceptable in all countries. The

coins are slightly difficult to tell apart when you're not used to them. The coppers are 1, 2 and 5 cent pieces, the golds are 10, 20 and 50, and the silver/gold combinations are €1 and €2.

ATMs and banks

The best way to get money in Spain is by plastic. ATMs are plentiful, and just about all of them accept all the major international debit and credit cards. The Spanish bank won't charge for the transaction, though they will charge a mark-up on the exchange rate, but beware of your own bank hitting you for a hefty fee: check with them before leaving home. Even if they do, it's likely to be a better deal than exchanging cash. The website www.moneysavingexpert.com has a good rundown on the most economical ways of accessing cash while travelling.

Banks are usually open Mon-Fri 0830-1400 (and Sat in winter) and many change foreign money (sometimes only the central branch in a town will do it). Commission rates vary widely; it's usually best to change large amounts, as there's often a minimum commission of €6 or so. Nevertheless, banks nearly always give better rates than change offices (*casas de cambio*), which are fewer by the day. If you're stuck outside banking hours, some large department stores such as El Corte Inglés change money at knavish rates.

Traveller's cheques are accepted in many shops, although they are far less common than they were.

Tax

Nearly all goods and services in Spain are subject to a value-added tax (IVA). This is currently 10% for most things the traveller will encounter, including restaurants and hotels, but is as high as 21% on some things. IVA is normally included in the stated prices. You're technically entitled to claim it back if you're a non-EU citizen, for purchases over €90. If you're buying something pricey, make sure you get a stamped receipt clearly showing the IVA component, as well as your name and passport number; you can claim the amount back at major airports on departure. Some shops will have a form to smooth the process.

Cost of living and travelling

Prices have soared since the euro was introduced; some basics rose by 50-80% in 3 years, and hotel and restaurant prices can seem dear even by Western European standards these days. Spain's average monthly salary of €1500 is low by EU standards, and the minimum monthly salary of €800 is very low indeed.

Spain can still be a reasonably cheap place to travel if you're prepared to forgo a few luxuries. If you're travelling as a pair, staying in cheap *pensiones*, eating a set meal at lunchtime, travelling short distances by bus or train daily, and snacking on tapas in the evenings, €70 per person per day is reasonable. If you camp and grab picnic lunches from shops, you could reduce this considerably. In a cheap hotel or good hostal and using a car, €130 a day and you'll not be counting pennies; €250 per day and you'll be very comfy indeed unless you're staying in 4- or 5-star accommodation.

Accommodation is more expensive in summer than in winter, although prices drop in Madrid in August when many businesses are closed and the city is stifling. The news isn't great for the solo traveller; single rooms tend not to be particularly good value, and they are in short supply. Prices range from 60-80% of the double/twin price; some places even charge the full rate. If you're going to be staying in 3- to 5-star hotels, booking them ahead on internet discount sites, such as www.booking.com or www.budgetplaces.com, can save a lot of money.

Public transport is generally cheap; intercity bus services are quick and low-priced and trains are reasonable, though the fast AVE trains cost substantially more.

Petrol is relatively cheap: standard unleaded petrol is around €1.38 per litre and diesel around €1.35. In some places, particularly in tourist areas, you may be charged up to 20% more to sit outside a restaurant. It's also worth checking if the 10% IVA (sales tax) is included in menu prices, especially in the more expensive restaurants; it should say on the menu whether this is the case.

Opening hours

Offices are usually open Mon-Fri 0800-1500. These hours might be official, but time in Spain is always fluid.

Safety

Spain is generally a safe place, with considerably less violent crime than many other European countries. However, street crime – bag-snatching and pickpocketing – in the bigger cities is on the rise. Don't invite crime by leaving luggage or cash in cars, and if you are parking in a city or a popular hiking zone, leave the glove box open so that thieves know there is nothing to steal.

There are several types of police, helpful enough in normal circumstances. The paramilitary Guardia Civil dress in green and are responsible for the roads (including speed traps and the like), borders and law enforcement away from towns. They're not a bunch to get the wrong side of but are polite to tourists and have thankfully lost the bizarre winged hats they used to sport. The Policía Nacional are responsible for most urban crimefighting. These are the ones to go to if you need to report anything stolen, etc. Policía Local/Municipal are present in large towns and cities and are responsible for some urban crime, as well as traffic control

and parking. Police stations are listed in phone books under *comisarías*. See also Insurance, page 21.

Telephone → *Country code +34.*
Phone booths on the street are mostly operated by Telefónica, and all have international direct dialling (00 is the prefix for international calls). They accept coins from €0.05 upwards and pre-paid phone cards, which can be bought from newsagents, post offices and tobacconists (*estancos*) in denominations of €5, 10, 15 and 20. Calls are cheaper after 2200 during the week and all day at weekends. Phones in bars and cafés usually have more expensive rates than public payphones. Phone centres (*locutorios*) are the cheapest method for calling abroad; you'll find them in the Atocha and Chamartín train stations, and several smaller ones dotted throughout Chueca and Lavapiés.

For directory enquiries, dial T11818 for national or T11825 for international numbers. (All these numbers are operated by Telefónica; other operators offer the same services).

Domestic landlines have 9-digit numbers beginning with 9 (occasionally with 8). Although the first 3 digits indicate the province, you have to dial the full number from wherever you are calling, including abroad. Mobiles numbers start with 6.

Mobiles (*móviles*) are big in Spain and coverage is very good. Most foreign mobiles will work in Spain; check with your service provider about what the call costs will be like. Many mobile networks require you to call up before leaving your home country to activate overseas service ('roaming'). If you're staying a while, it may be cheaper to buy a Spanish mobile or SIM card, as there are always numerous offers and discounts. You could even purchase a 'disposable' BIC mobile phone at several outlets including **Schleker**. They cost about €20 and include €12 of calls.

Time

Spain operates on western European time, ie GMT +1, and changes its clocks in line with the rest of the EU.

'Spanish time' isn't as elastic as it used to be, but if you're told something will happen 'en seguida' ('straight away') it may take 10 mins, if you're told 'cinco minutos' (5 mins), grab a seat and a book. Transport, especially buses, leaves promptly.

Tipping

Tipping in Spain is far from compulsory, but much practised. Around 10% is considered fairly generous in a restaurant; 3-5% is more usual. It's rare for a service charge to be added to a bill. Waiters do not normally expect tips for lunchtime set meals or tapas, but here and in bars and cafés people will often leave small change, especially for table service. Taxi drivers don't expect a tip, but don't expect you to sit around waiting for twenty cents change either. In rural areas, churches will often have a local keyholder who will open it up for you; if there's no admission charge, a tip or donation is appropriate; say €1 per head; more if they've given a detailed tour.

Toilets

Public toilets are not common, although you'll find them in train stations. It's usually okay to use the ones in bars and cafés. You might have to use the bin next to the loo for your toilet paper if the system can't cope, particularly in out-of-the-way places. There are usually toilets in the big department stores, too.

Tourist information → *See individual entries for specific details of tourist offices.*

The tourist information infrastructure in Spain is organized by the regional governments and is generally excellent, with a wide range of information, often in English, German and French as well as Spanish. Offices within the region can provide maps of the area and towns, and lists of registered accommodation, usually with a booklet for hotels, *hostales*, and *pensiones*; another for campsites, and another, especially worth picking up, listing farmstay and rural accommodation, which has taken off in a big way; hundreds are added yearly. Opening hours are longer in major cities; many rural offices are only open in summer. Average opening hours are Mon-Sat 1000-1400, 1600-1900, Sun 1000-1400. Offices are often closed on Sun or Mon. Staff often speak English and other European languages

Visas and immigration

Entry requirements are subject to change, so always check with the Spanish tourist board or an embassy/consulate if you're not an EU citizen. EU citizens and those from countries within the Schengen agreement can enter Spain freely. UK/Irish citizens will need to carry a passport, while an identity card suffices for other EU/Schengen nationals. Citizens of Australia, the USA, Canada, New Zealand and Israel can enter without a visa for up to 90 days. Other citizens will require a visa, obtainable from Spanish consulates or embassies. These are usually issued very quickly and valid for all Schengen countries. The basic visa is valid for 90 days, and you'll need 2 passport photos, proof of funds covering your stay, and possibly evidence of medical cover (ie insurance). For extensions of visas, apply to an *oficina de extranjeros* in a major city.

Weights and measures

The Spanish use the metric system. Decimal places are indicated with commas, and thousands with points.

Contents

26 Madrid
27 Arriving in Madrid
28 *Map: Madrid*
30 Old Madrid
32 *Map: Madrid centre*
35 Plaza de Oriente and the Palacio Real
38 Plaza de Santa Ana and around
40 Prado and Triángulo del Arte
45 Around the Prado
48 La Latina and Lavapíes
51 Gran Vía, Chueca and Malasaña
55 Salamanca
57 Ventas
58 Listings

74 Central Spain
75 Getting around
75 El Escorial and the Sierra de Guadarrama
77 Segovia and around
78 *Map: Segovia*
82 Ávila
84 *Map: Ávila*
86 Sierra de Gredos
88 Alcalá de Henares and around
89 Aranjuez
90 Chinchón
91 Toledo
92 *Map: Toledo*
98 Listings

Footprint features

27 Arriving late at Madrid Barajas
41 Highlights of Paseo del Arte
49 Being Madrileño
53 El Dos de Mayo
65 One-stop-shop...
69 Zarzuela
83 Something in the air

Madrid & Central Spain

Madrid

Madrid was an uneventful country town back in 1561 when Felipe II proclaimed it Spain's new capital. Set high on a baking plain, the city appealed to Felipe because it was slap-bang in the centre of Spain (although the excellence of the hunting may also have had something to do with what everyone agreed was an idiosyncratic choice). Its Golden Age was the 17th century, when gold and silver poured in from Mexico and Peru, Cervantes published *Don Quixote* and Velázquez was appointed court painter to the Habsburg kings.

Nowadays the city has a split personality: on the one hand it's the political, artistic and royal centre of Spain with all the fancy trimmings; on the other, it's an overgrown market town where everyone knows everyone else's business. And they will want to know yours too – the Madrileños are famous all over Spain for their directness (or rudeness, according to some from out of town). This is simply a desire not to waste time on small talk, but to concentrate hard on the real business of having a good time. This is where the Madrileños excel, and there can be few cities in the world which radiate such vitality. There are thousands of tapas bars, flamenco clubs, cafés, and *terrazas*, but it's in the packed streets – especially just after El Rastro flea market, or in the early hours of a hot summer's night – that the uniquely Madrileño gift for enjoying life really shines out.

Arriving late at Madrid Barajas

If you arrive at Madrid airport in the middle of the night, few services will be open. The cafeteria in Terminal 1 closes at 2330, and the shops, post office and information desks usually close at around 2200 or earlier.

If you have pre-booked a car, some car hire representatives will meet your flight whenever it arrives, but you should check this in advance.

There are a couple of expensive business hotels close to the airport. The metro runs until about midnight during the week or 0100 at weekends, and the airport bus runs until 0145. Taxis can be found outside the arrival halls; if you can't see one, call Radio Taxis on T915 478 500/915 478 600.

If you haven't booked accommodation, your best bet is to head for an area hostels clustered on one street (such as Calle Hortaleza in Chueca, or the streets around the Plaza de Santa Ana, see Where to stay, page 58). If you can't afford a taxi, you'll have little choice but to wait it out at the airport until 0445 when the buses start running into the city again. Still, the airport is clean and safe, and there are snack and drink machines to keep you going.

Arriving in Madrid

Getting there

Madrid's international airport is in Barajas, 13 km northeast of the city. The main bus and coach station for national and international buses in Madrid is the Estación Sur de Autobuses, Calle Méndez Alvaro, T914 684 200 (Metro Méndez Alvaro). Bus 148 or the metro will link you with Plaza Colón in the city centre. There are two main train stations in Madrid: Atocha in the south of the city, and Chamartín in the north. Both are large, modern and well-equipped, with shops, cafés, ATMs and car-rental services. Both are linked to the centre of the city (Atocha is pretty central anyway) by metro. ▸▸ *See Getting to Madrid and Central Spain, page 6, and Transport, page 72.*

Getting around → *The city information line (T010) will also give out transport information.*

Bus and metro plans are available at tourist offices, at metro and bus stations, or online at www.ctm-madrid.es (which also provides information on suburban bus and rail services if you are planning a day trip to Toledo or Segovia, for example). Driving in Madrid is a nightmare and entirely unnecessary given the excellence of the public transport. Madrid is best seen on foot. The centre is relatively small and most of the sights are within easy walking distance of each other. It's easy to get lost but that is half the charm. Free maps are provided by tourist offices, and there's a good selection of better maps at most bookshops (see page 70). ▸▸ *For tours see What to do, page 71; see also Transport, page 72.*

Orientation

The heart of Madrid is tiny, a medieval kernel of narrow streets spidering off small squares under a crooked skyline of spires and cupolas. The oldest part of the city is the area around the **Plaza Mayor** and the Royal Palace, with twisting alleys and traditional shops and bars. To the east is the old literary *barrio* of **Santa Ana**, now best known for its nightlife and tapas bars, and east again is the elegant **Paseo del Prado**, where the Prado

1 Madrid

➡ Madrid maps
1 Madrid, page 28
2 Madrid centre, page 32
See page 30 for the key

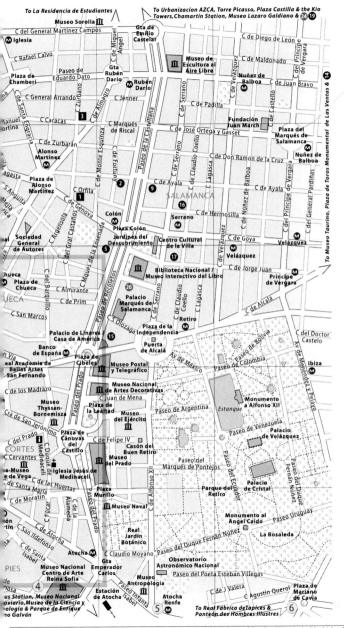

To La Residencia de Estudiantes
Museo Sorolla
C del General Martínez Campos
Iglesia
C Rafael Calvo
Plaza de Chamberí
Paseo de Eduardo Dato
C General Arrando
C de Santa Engracia
C Caracas
Manuel Cortina
C de Zurbarán
Alonso Martínez
Plaza de Alonso Martínez
C de Genova
C del Gral Castaños
Orfila
Sociedad General de Autores
Chueca
Plaza de Chueca
CHUECA
C del Barquillo
C Almirante
C de Prim
C San Marcos
Palacio de Linares / Casa de América
Banco de España
Plaza de Cibeles
Real Academia de Bellas Artes San Fernando
C de los Madrazo
Museo Thyssen-Bornemisza
Cta de San Jerónimo
Plaza de Cánovas del Castillo
CORTES
Cervantes
Casa-Museo de Vega
Medinaceli
C de las Huertas
Iglesia Jesús de Medinaceli
C de Santa María
C de Moratín
C San Ildefonso
C de la Alameda
C de Santa Isabel
PIES
Museo Nacional Centro de Arte Reina Sofía
Atocha
Gta Emperador Carlos
Estación de Atocha
Bus Station, Museo Nacional Ferroviario, Museo de la Ciencia y Tecnología & Parque de Enrique Tierno Galván

To Urbanizacion AZCA, Torre Picasso, Plaza Castilla & the Kio Towers, Chamartín Station, Museo Lázaro Galdiano & 24 19
Gta de Emilio Castelar
C de Diego de León
C del General Martínez Campos
C de Maldonado
C de Miguel Ángel
Gta Rubén Darío
Rubén Darío
Museo de Escultura al Aire Libre
C de Velázquez
Núñez de Balboa
C de Juan Bravo
C de Zurbano
C de Almagro
C de Fortuny
C Jenner
C de Padilla
Fundación Juan March
Plaza del Marqués de Salamanca
C Marqués de Riscal
C de José Ortega y Gasset
C de Serrano
C de Claudio Coello
Núñez de Balboa
C de Don Ramón de la Cruz
C de Monte Esquinza
Paseo de la Castellana
C de Ayala
C de Ayala
C de Núñez de Balboa
C de Príncipe de Vergara
C de General Pardiñas
SALAMANCA
C de Lagasca
C de Hermosilla
Serrano
Centro Cultural de la Villa
Colón
Plaza Colón
Jardines del Descubrimiento
C de Goya
Velázquez
Biblioteca Nacional / Museo Interactivo del Libro
C de Jorge Juan
Príncipe de Vergara
Palacio Marqués de Salamanca
Retiro
C de Claudio Coello
C de Lagasca
C de Alcalá
Paseo de Recoletos
C de Olózaga
Plaza de la Independencia
Puerta de Alcalá
Av de México
Paseo de Colombia
Paseo de Bolivia
C del Doctor Castelo
Ibiza
Museo Postal y Telegráfico
Museo Nacional de Artes Decorativas
C Juan de Mena
Paseo del Prado
Plaza de la Lealtad
Museo del Ejército
Paseo de Argentina
Estanque
Monumento a Alfonso XII
C de Felipe IV
Casón del Buen Retiro
Museo del Prado
Paseo de Venezuela
Palacio de Velázquez
Paseo del Duque Fernán Núñez
Paseo del Marqués de Pontejos
Paseo del Ecuador
Parque del Retiro
Palacio de Cristal
Plaza Murillo
Museo Naval
Paseo de Alfonso XII
Real Jardín Botánico
Monumento al Ángel Caído
Paseo Uruguay
La Rosaleda
C Claudio Moyano
Paseo del Duque Fernán Núñez
Observatorio Astronómico Nacional
Museo Antropología
Paseo del Poeta Esteban Villegas
C de Valera
C Agustín Querol
Plaza de Mariano de Cavia
Gta Infanta Isabel
Atocha Renfe
To Real Fábrica de Tapices & Panteón des Hombres Ilustres

Madrid key

Where to stay ▣
Orfila **1** *B4*
Santo Mauro **3** *A4*

Restaurants ●
Bar Casa do
  Compañeiro **1** *B3*
Bar Tomate **2** *B5*
Bodegas El Maño **7** *B2*
Café Comercial **3** *B3*
Café de Ruiz **4** *B3*

Café del Espejo **5** *C5*
Café Manuela **6** *B3*
El Jardín Secreto **8** *B2*
Embassy **9** *B5*
La Cabrera **15** *C5*
La Isla del Tesoro **11** *B3*
La Musa **12** *B3*
Los Timbales **14** *A6*
Teatriz **16** *B5*
Thai Gardens **17** *C5*
Zalacaín **19** *A6*

Bars & clubs ♥
Alquimia **20** *C5*
El Café de la Palma **22** *B2*
Lolita Lounge
  & Bar **24** *A6*

forms one point of the world-famous **Triangulo del Arte**. South of the Plaza Mayor are the shabby, bohemian neighbourhoods of **La Latina** and **Lavapiés**, and to the north is the wide, flashy **Gran Vía**, which cuts from east to west across the northern strip of the city. Madrid's trendiest neighbourhoods – **Chueca** and **Malasaña** – sit to the north of the Gran Vía. East of Chueca is the elegant 19th-century grid of **Salamanca**, Madrid's answer to London's Knightsbridge or New York's Upper West Side, and the **Paseo de la Castellana** runs north of here, lined with glassy skyscrapers and banks. Most of the sights are within strolling distance of each other, and those that aren't are easily accessibly by the cheap, efficient and easy-to-use metros and buses.

Tourist information

Madrid's tourist information offices can provide you with a basic plan of the city, and a copy of *What's On*, a pocket-sized magazine with helpful local information and listings (also available online at www.esmadrid.com). Pick up the free English-language monthly newspaper *InMadrid*, www.inmadrid.com, with plenty of bar and club listings. There is a tourist information line, T902 100 007, and a city information line, T010, both of which usually have English-speaking operators. There are two official websites: www.turismo madrid.es, run by the regional authority, and www.esmadrid.com, run by the city.

The main **city tourist information** is at ① *Plaza Mayor 27, T914 544 410, www.esmadrid.com, daily 0900-2030*. There are other branches at the Plaza de Colón, open daily 0900-2030; the airport (terminals 2 and 4); and the information points at the Paseo del Arte (near the Prado) and the Plaza de Callao (on the Gran Vía). The main **regional tourist office** is at ① *C/del Duque de Medinaceli, 2, T914 294 951, Mon-Fri 0900-1900, Sat 0900-1300*.

Old Madrid → *For listings, see pages 58-72.*

The oldest part of the Madrid lies between the Puerta del Sol on the east and the enormous Palacio Real (Royal Place) on the west surrounded with manicured gardens and graceful squares. In the middle is the Plaza Mayor, easily the grandest square in all Madrid, completely enclosed, and surrounded with elegant arcades. The Madrileños have all but abandoned it to tourists, but it's still a handsome spot for a coffee out on the terrace. The area around it is known as Habsburg Madrid, or Madrid of the Austrias, and the winding streets and passages are sprinkled with old palaces and monasteries, tiny churches and traditional shops selling handmade guitars, religious goods, or fine wines. Its proximity to the royal palace has meant that this neighbourhood has always been pretty fancy – at least until the posh families moved out to the grand new avenues of Salamanca a century or so ago – and the restaurants and smart tapas bars are a cut above the workaday places in other parts of the city.

Puerta del Sol

① *This is the crossroads of Madrid, the meeting point of 10 major roads and shopping streets.*
The 'Gate of the Sun' was once one of the entrance gates to the city back when it was still surrounded by walls. Now this elliptical square is disappointingly bland, and, although there is a constant flow of people, they are always on their way somewhere else. It wasn't always this way: the Puerta del Sol used to be the most piquant neighbourhood in Madrid, where you could pick up an assassin or a whore or just catch up with the latest gossip from the court. Even a century ago, the square's animation was legendary but now there is little to detain anyone besides the 19th-century pastry shop at No 2, **La Mallorquina**.

The grand, pinkish building on one side of the square (now government offices) has a plaque outside it which marks the very centre of Spain – '**Kilometre Zero**' – from which all distances are measured. This is also where Madrileños gather to bring in the New Year, traditionally eating one grape at each chime of the bell from the clock tower. Opposite the post office is the bronze state of Madrid's symbol, the '**bear and the madroño tree**', which is a popular meeting place. No one quite knows how this unlikely pair came to symbolize the city, and the legends which now surround it are disappointingly prosaic – it seems most likely that the madroño tree shares the first part of its name with Madrid, and that the region was once full of bears.

Plaza Mayor and around

If you want to see what a madroño tree looks like, the council have planted several along the **Calle Mayor**, which runs off to the east of the Puerta del Sol and was once the most important street in Madrid. There's nothing much to see nowadays besides chain stores and banks, but it leads to the city's grandest square, the Plaza Mayor. This vast cobbled square is surrounded by lofty arcades and tall mansions topped with steep slate roofs. Bright and sunny, it's packed with terrace cafés, souvenir shops, and sun-worshipping tourists – the only time you might catch a Madrileño here is on a Sunday morning when a stamp and coin market is held under the arcades.

The square was built by Juan Gómez de Mora to designs conceived by Felipe II's favourite architect, Juan de Herrera. This was the ceremonial centre of Madrid, a magnificent backdrop for coronations, executions, markets, bullfights and fiestas. It is riddled with the subterranean torture chambers of the Inquisition, who used the square for *autos-da-fé* – the trial of suspected heretics. In just one day in 1680, they tried 118 prisoners here, and burned 21 of them alive. Before the square was built, a market was traditionally held in front of the **Casa de la Panadería**, the old bakery, which is now the most eye-catching building on the square. It was repainted in 1992 by Carlos Franco who covered it with a hippy-trippy fresco of floating nymphs.

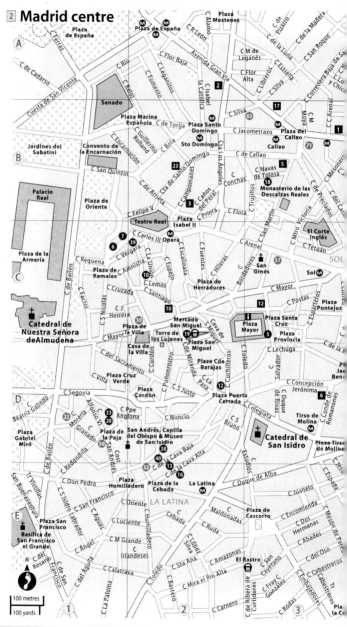

② Madrid centre

Plaza de España
Plaza Mostenes
C R León
Plaza de España
C Álamo
C de Pizarro
C de la Madera
C de la Luna
C San Roque

Ferraz
C de Cadarso
Avenida Gran Vía
C Flor Baja
C Legan itos
C Fomento
C Río
C Reloj
C Isabel la Católica
C M de Leganés
C Flor Alta
Corredera Baja de San
y Chice
C Libreros
C Estrella
C Silva
C M Moya

Cuesta de San Vicente
Senado
C de Torija
Plaza Marina Española
Plaza Santo Domingo
Sto Domingo
C Jacometrazo
C Silva
Plaza del Callao
C Arenal

Jardines del Sabatini
Convento de la Encarnación
C Guillermo Rolland
C Bola
C de los Angeles
Callao
C de Callao
Navas de Tolosa

C San Quintín
Cta de Santo Domingo
Campomanes
Caños del Peral
Conchas
Monasterio de las Descalzas Reales

Palacio Real
Plaza de Oriente
C de Arrieta
C Felipe V
C Priora
C Flora

Plaza de la Armería
Teatro Real
Plaza Isabel II
C San Martín
El Corte Inglés

Catedral de Nuestra Señora de Almudena
C Carlos III
Opera
C Vergara
C Espejo
C Escalinata
C Fuentes
C Hileras
C Arenal
C Tetuán

C de Bailén
C Requena
Plaza de Ramales
C Amnistía
C Lepanto
C Lemos
C Santiago
Plaza de Herradores
San Ginés
Sol

C Factor
C Nicolás
C J Herrera
Plaza de la Villa
C Mayor
Mercado San Miguel
Plaza San Miguel
Cava de San Miguel
Plaza Mayor
Plaza Santa Cruz
Plaza Provincia
C Postas
Plaza Pontejos

Catedral de Nuestra Señora de Almudena
Casa de la Villa
Torre de los Lujanes
C de Miranda
Plaza Cde Barajas
C Toledo
C Lechuga

C del Sacramento
C Córdon
Plaza Cruz Verde
C Puñonrostro
C La Pasa
C S Justo
Plaza Puerta Cerrada
C Concepción Jerónima
C Duque de Rivas

C Segovia
Beatriz Galindo
C Ppe Anglona
C Nuncio
Colegiata
Tirso de Molina
Plaza Tirso de Molina

C Morería
Alfonso VI
C Granado
Plaza de la Paja
San Andrés, Capilla del Obispo & Museo de San Isidro
C S Bruno
Catedral de San Isidro

Plaza Gabriel Miró
C Redondilla
C Don Pedro
C San Andrés
C de la Cava Baja
C de la Cava Alta
Estudios
C Duque de Alba
Juanelo

Plaza San Francisco
Basílica de San Francisco el Grande
C del Rosario
C de San Francisco
C de San Isidro Labrador
C Aguas
Plaza Humilladero
Plaza de la Cebada
La Latina
Plaza de Cascorro
C Encomienda
C Dos Hermanas

C del Ángel
C M Grande
LA LATINA
C Cebada
C Maldonadas
C Abades
C del Oso

C Calatrava
C Luciente
C Humilladero
C López Silva
C Sta Ana
C Ruda
C Amazonas
El Rastro
C San Cayetano
C Fray C González
C Cabestreros

C La Paloma
C del Águila
C Toledo
C Bastero
C Mira el Río Alta
C de Ribera de Curtidores
C Carnero
C Rodas

100 metres
100 yards

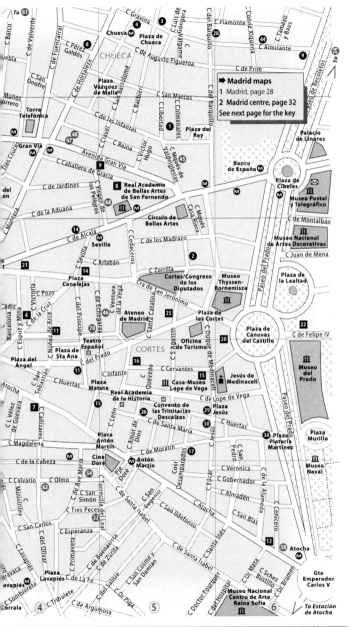

➡ Madrid maps
1 Madrid, page 28
2 Madrid centre, page 32
See next page for the key

Madrid centre key

Where to stay 📷
Atlántico **1** *B3*
Chic & Basic Mayerling **6** *D3*
De las Letras H&R **9** *B5*
Emperador **2** *A2*
Hostal Adriá
 Santa Ana **11** *C4*
Hostal Adriano **4** *C4*
Hostal Conchita **5** *B3*
Hostal Fonda
 Horizonte **7** *D4*
Hostal Hispano
 Argentino **8** *B5*
Hostal Pinariega **10** *C2*
Hostel Astoria **14** *C4*
Hostel Cervantes **15** *D5*
Hostel Jaen **16** *D5*
Hostel Lauria **17** *B3*
Husa Paseo del Arte **12** *E6*
Palace **20** *C6*
París **21** *C4*
Plaza Mayor **12** *C3*
Ritz **22** *C6*
Room Mate Mario **3** *B2*
Tryp Ambassador **23** *B2*
Villa Real **25** *C5*

Restaurants 🍴
Bar Manolo **2** *C5*
Bocaíto **1** *B5*
Bodegas de Ángel
 Sierra **3** *A5*
Café Acuarela **4** *A5*
Café de los
 Austrias **6** *C1*
Café de Oriente **7** *C1*
Café Figueroa **8** *A4*
Café Gijón **9** *A6*
Café La Union **10** *C2*
Café Oliver **44** *A6*
Casa Alberto **11** *D4*
Casa Botín **12** *D2*
Casa Lucio **13** *E2*
Casa María **5** *C3*
Champanería
 Gala **17** *D5*
Cornucopia **18** *B3*
El Estragón **20** *D1*
El Pez Gordo **21** *A3*
La Biotika **26** *D5*
La Castafiore **28** *A6*
La Dolores **29** *D5*
La Fábrica **30** *D5*
La Musa Latina **33** *D1*
La Platería **34** *D6*
La Terraza del Casino **14** *C4*

Le Petit Bistrot **15** *D4*
Matritum **16** *E2*
Taberna del Cruzado **39** *C2*
Mercado San Miguel **19** *C2*
Taberna Almendro **38** *D2*
Taberna Tempranillo **40** *D2*

Bars & clubs 🍸
Aloque **22** *E4*
Belmondo **23** *D1*
Camp **45** *B5*
Cardamomo **46** *C5*
Chicote **47** *B4*
Club Ventura **62** *E4*
Cock **48** *B4*
Delic **50** *D1*
El Bonnano **52** *E2*
El Mojito **54** *E4*
Goa/Ohm/Bash **71** *B3*
Joy Eslava **57** *C3*
Kapital **58** *E6*
Kathmandu **59** *C2*
La Ida **61** *A4*
Larios Café **63** *B3*
Serrano 41 **24** *A6*
Suite Café-Club **68** *B5*
Viva Madrid **70** *C4*

Arched passages lead off the Plaza Mayor to some of the most important streets of 17th-century Madrid – Calle Toledo, Calle Mayor, and Calle Segovia – as well as several which still echo the trades which were once carried out here, like Calle Cuchilleros (the Street of the Knife-Sharpeners), which incorporates part of the old city walls. This is where you'll find the traditional *mesones*, or inns, which grew up to cater to merchants and travellers arriving at the city gates. **Casa Botín** (see page 60) opened in the 16th century and claims to be the oldest restaurant in the world. Calle Cuchilleros heads up to meet the Plaza San Miguel, with Madrid's prettiest covered market at the centre. **Mercado de San Miguel**, an airy glass and wrought-iron pavilion designed by a pupil of Gustave Eiffel, is now a temple to gastronomy, full of gourmet shops, tapas bars and stalls selling specialist produce.

Plaza de la Villa and around

Continuing down the Calle Mayor once again, there's another handsome square on the left. The small, austere Plaza de la Villa is one of the oldest squares in Madrid, and is overlooked by the **Casa de la Villa** (City Hall), which was begun in 1640 to plans drawn up by Juan Gómez de Moro. Until then, the city was small enough to be managed with the odd council meeting held in a local church. By 1640, it was felt that something a little more imposing was in order for what was, after all, the capital of an empire. Even though the City Hall moved to the old post office (Palacio de las Comunicaciones, on Plaza de

Cibeles; see page 45), the building is still open for guided visits, but there's nothing especially interesting to see besides the plush Salón de Sesiones where city matters are deliberated in a whirl of velvet and gilt.

Opposite the Casa de la Villa is the **Torre de los Lujanes**, the oldest secular building in Madrid, although it's been restored almost beyond recognition. At the corner of tiny Calle del Codo, you can just make out a Moorish archway incorporated into the walls. (If you duck down this little alley, you can pick up some cakes at the **Convento de las Carboneras**, see page 71). The handsome 16th-century palace which stands beyond the Casa de la Villa and closes off the square was home to Cardenal Cisneros, founder of the famous university in Alcalá de Henares (see page 88).

Calle Arenal to the Plaza de Oriente

Another of the main roads splintering westwards from the Puerta del Sol, Calle Arenal was one of the main processional routes of Habsburg Madrid, lined with convents, palaces and churches. Now it's mainly a shopping street, with a smattering of bars, cafés and clubs. Tucked back half-way along it on the left, the **Iglesia de San Ginés** is a gloomy 17th-century church which reeks of incense, and is run by the shadowy ultra-reactionary Opus Dei. There's a version of El Greco's *The Purification of the Temple* in a small side chapel, but it's only open during services.

Almost opposite the church, the Calle San Martín leads to the **Monasterio de las Descalzas Reales** ① *Plaza de las Descalzas Reales 3, T914 548 800, Metro Sol or Opera, Tue-Sat 1000-1400 and 1600-1830, Sun 1000-1500, €7/€4 concessions (€10 including visit to Monasterio de la Encarnación; also €25 for Madrid Capital Bono 48 hr, which allows access to 5 major sites in 2 days), free to EU-passport holders on Wed and Thu afternoons, visits by guided tour only – officially in Spanish, although guides are often multilingual.* The Royal Monastery of Poor Clares was founded by Juana of Austria, daughter of Carlos I (Charles V), who was born here in its former incarnation as a royal palace. Widowed at the age of 19, she established this convent for aristocratic nuns and widows. Thanks to its royal connections, it became one of the richest religious institutions in the kingdom, crammed with paintings, tapestries and ornaments – although most were later sold when the convent fell on hard times. There is still a community of nuns here, who care for the pretty kitchen gardens and orchard which can be glimpsed from the windows. The opulent main staircase survived the transition from palace to convent, and is thickly covered in trompe l'oeil frescoes, including a delightful one of Felipe IV and his family gathered on a balcony. The highlight of the convent visit is the remarkable collection of tapestries, particularly a 17th-century series called the *Triumph of the Eucharist* which was designed by Rubens and woven in Brussels. This is where you'll find the only mirror in the whole convent, used to show off the sketch on the back of one of the tapestries. Downstairs is a recreation of a cell, complete with the spiked sandals and knotted rope which the nuns used to mortify their flesh, and some painting galleries; most are copies or minor works, but the nuns have managed to hang on to a Titian, a portrait of San Francisco by Zurbarán, and a small Virgin by Luis Morales.

Plaza de Oriente and the Palacio Real

The Calle Arenal continues westwards and widens into the **Plaza Isabel II**, a transport hub for buses and metros, which is overlooked by the imposing back entrance to the Teatro

Real (see below). Pedestrian alleys on either side of the Teatro lead to the delightful Plaza de Oriente, a half-moon shaped square, with manicured gardens, statues and elegant terrace cafés. It was built by Joseph Bonaparte, Napoleon's brother, who was given the nickname *El Rey Plazuelas* (King of the Squares) for his habit of knocking down jumbles of old buildings and replacing them with public squares. In the centre is a 17th-century equestrian statue of Felipe IV, which posed problems for its sculptor, Petro Tacca, until Galileo suggested he balance the horse by making the back from solid bronze and keeping the front hollow.

Teatro Real

ⓘ *Plaza de Oriente s/n, T915 160 696, www.teatro-real.com, open for guided visits daily 1030-1300, closed Aug, €7/€12/€16. For box office ticket sales, T902 244 848.*

The Royal Theatre, Madrid's beautiful opera house, flanks one side of the square. Completed in time for Isabel II's 20th birthday celebrations in 1850, this is where the Madrileños were introduced to the works of Verdi, Wagner and Stravinsky, along with daring new ballets by Diaghilev and the Ballet Russe. But the theatre was closed in 1925 and only finally reopened in 1997 after a massive facelift which included the addition of state-of-the-art technology. Three kinds of visits are available: the standard visits are the shortest, but artistic and technical visits are available if you're in interested in seeing behind the scenes.

Palacio Real

ⓘ *C/Bailén s/n, T915 420 059, Metro Opera, daily 1000-1800, Apr-Sep until 2000, €10, €17 with guided tour, €14 with audio guide, €5 concessions, free to EU-passport holders on Wed and Thu afternoons. The palace is still used for official functions and can be closed at short notice – if 2 flags are flying instead of just one, the king is at home and you won't be allowed in.*

The Teatro Real is dwarfed by the other enormous edifice which flanks the Plaza de Oriente: the Royal Palace built by the Bourbons in the 1730s to replace the *alcázar* (fortress) which had done service as a royal residence since Moorish times. When the fortress was destroyed by fire in 1734, Felipe V saw an opportunity for something altogether grander, and commissioned the most prestigious architects of the day to create this monumental pile. Built on a staggering scale – thankfully, earlier plans for a palace four times the size of the current one were rejected – it's undoubtedly imposing, but it's no surprise that Juan Carlos I and his family have chosen to live in the more modest surroundings of the Palacio de Zarzuela on the outskirts of Madrid.

The visit begins with Francisco Sabatini's icy staircase of pale marble which leads up to the main floor and the Salón de los Alabarderos (Hall of the Halbardiers), where there's a magnificent ceiling fresco by the Venetian painter, Tiepolo, who came to Madrid at the age of 62. The most sumptuous room in the palace is the Throne Room, finished in 1772, and densely upholstered in deep red velvet and gold, with Tiepolo's last masterpiece, *The Majesty of the Spanish Monarchy*, spreading dramatically across the vast ceiling. Many of the chambers are lined with tapestries made in the Real Fabrica de Tapices but most of the paintings are copies – the originals, including Goya's portraits of Charles IV and his wife María Luisa, are exhibited at the Prado. One of the most eye-popping rooms is the Porcelain Room, encrusted with 134 oriental porcelain panels and silk hangings. Other highlights include the exceptional collection of musical instruments in the Stradivarius room – some dating back to the 17th century, many with exquisite decorative detail –

and the collection of royal porcelain and crystal from the royal factories in the Buen Retiro and elsewhere. Highlights of the royal art collection can be seen in the Painting Galleries.

Plaza de la Armería

Off the enormous Plaza de la Armería are two small royal museums (admission included in entrance ticket); the most entertaining is the **Royal Armoury**, where El Cid's legendary sword is given pride of place. There is a huge selection of armour – including armour for horses and even an elegant outfit for Carlos I's (Charles V) hunting dog. Across the square, the **Royal Pharmacy** has a recreated 19th-century pharmacy complete with porcelain jars and fittings.

Palace gardens

The palace gardens are a good place to recover from the excess of gilt and marble: the largest is the **Parque-Jardín El Campo del Moro** ① *Paseo Virgen del Puerto s/n, El Campo de Moro, daily 0900-dusk, free,* which spreads downhill to the Manzanares River, but you'll have to walk all the way around to the entrance on the Paseo Virgen del Puerto to get in. They offer spectacular views up to the palace. Equally lovely and more easily accessible are the **Jardins del Sabatini** to the north of the palace, which are very small but beautifully laid out with fountains and shady paths.

As if the Palacio Real wasn't big enough and glittering enough to satisfy any wannabe prince or princess, construction is underway just outside the main gates of the palace on a huge, new museum which will house the 'Royal Collections'. The boxy, contemporary construction is built over the remains of the original *alcázar* or fortress which first occupied the site, and will provide a home for about 150,000 artworks – many of which have never been displayed before. Among the highlights will be an entire gallery dedicated to the royal collection of tapestries, as well as a display of lavish ceremonial carriages dating back centuries.

Catedral de Nuestra Señora de la Almudena

① *C/Bailén, T915 422 200, Metro Opera, Mon-Sat 1000-1330, 1800-2000, Sun 1000-1400, 1800-2045, free; museum and dome €6. Mass is held daily at 1000 and 1200, Sun 1030, 1200, 1800 and 1900.*

Right opposite the entrance to the Royal Palace, there's no missing the huge concrete lump which is the Catedral de Nuestra Señora de la Almudena, Madrid's first cathedral. Right up until 1993, when it was opened amid much pomp and ceremony (and a shower of confetti made with telephone directories) by Pope John Paul II, Madrid was part of the diocese of Toledo and had no cathedral to call its own. Plans for converting the former church of Our Lady of the Almudena into a cathedral were drawn up in the 1870s, but, despite more than a century of work, the finished product is banal. Much more atmospheric is the crypt (entrance around the corner on Calle Mayor), which was the first part to be completed, and has a creepy charm of its own. The views from the **dome**, however, are fantastic.

Convento de la Encarnación

① *Plaza de la Encarnación 1, T914 548 800, www.patrimonionacional.es, Metro Opera. Visits by guided tour only (Spanish only, 40 mins) Tue-Sat 1000-1400, 1600-1830, €7/€4 or (or €10 combined ticket with Monasterio de les Descalzas Reales; or €25 for the Madrid Capital Bono 48 hr, which gives admissions to 5 major sites over 2 days).*

A two-minute stroll north of the Plaza de Oriente, is another of Madrid's quirky convents – the Convento de la Encarnación – which opened its doors to the public in the 1980s. Like other religious institutions, it has had to find new ways of funding itself in post-Franco Spain. The convent was commissioned by Margaret of Austria, consort to Felipe II, and was once connected to the Royal Alcázar (which preceded the present Royal Palace, see above) by a long corridor. It looks modest enough on the outside, but parts of the predominantly Baroque interior are still fit for kings. The highlight of the tour is the final room, the Reliquario, a subterranean, dimly lit room lined with cabinets stuffed with the relics of thousands of saints – nails, skulls, hair, crumbling bones, and phials of blood all wrapped in garlands and displayed in intricate cases. Madrid's most famous relic is housed here, a tiny flask containing the blood of San Pantaleón which miraculously liquefies each year on the day of his martyrdom, 27 July. According to legend, if it liquefies at any other time, the country is in danger.

Plaza de Santa Ana and around

Just behind the Puerta del Sol is the enticing web of streets around the Plaza de Santa Ana, an engaging neighbourhood of blind alleys, leaning houses and old-fashioned shops which attracts twice as many tourists as locals. It's always been the entertainment district – now it's the bars and restaurants which draw the crowds, but once it was theatres and whorehouses. On the fringes of this bohemian *barrio* is the decidedly un-bohemian Cortes (Parliament) and the sticky-sweet delights of some of Madrid's oldest patisseries.

Plaza de Santa Ana

Plaza de Santa Ana, surrounded by bars, restaurants, theatres and hotels, has been the heart of this neighbourhood for centuries. The pavements are lined with terraces from the dozens of bars, many of which are filled with tiles and turn-of-the-century fittings, and it's one of the most popular places in Madrid for the *tapeo* (a pub crawl from tapas bar to tapas bar). The square is overlooked by the **Teatro Español**, an 18th-century theatre which has seen some important premieres, including the first rowdy production of Lorca's *Yerma* in 1934, when the outraged audience screamed out 'queer' and 'whore' throughout the performance.

Opposite the theatre is a Belle Epoque-style hotel, now the fashionable **Hotel Me**, which was a favourite with bullfighters in its earlier incarnation. It has a plaque to Manolete, perhaps the most famous *torero* of all time, just outside the entrance.

Ateneo Artístico, Científico y Literario de Madrid
ⓘ *C/Prado 21, not open to the public.*
A stroll down the Calle del Prado from the Plaza de Santa Ana passes the entrance to **Calle Echegaray**, named for an almost-forgotten Nobel prize-winner, which is crammed with old-fashioned bars tiled from floor to ceiling. Further down on the left you'll find the Ateneo Artístico, Científico y Literario de Madrid, which was established in 1820 as a patriotic society for the advancement of arts, literature and sciences, and so naturally it was almost immediately closed down by the repressive King Ferdinand VII who mistrusted anything which smacked of Liberalism. On Ferdinand's death in 1835, it reopened in the Calle del Prado which was then lined with cafés popular with writers and

intellectuals, and has been housed in this elegant late 19th-century building since the 1880s. Officially it's only open to members but it's occasionally possible to sweet-talk the doormen into letting you in to see the glorious old library, one of Spain's finest, which exudes a dusty, tranquil air of scholarship.

Casa-Museo Lope de Vega

① *C/Cervantes, T914 299 216, Metro Antón Martín, Tue-Sun 1000-1500, tours by guided visit only (Spanish), free.*

The neighbourhood's literary tradition stretches back several centuries before the arrival of the Ateneo. One of Spain's best-known writers is Lope de Vega, whose house, the Casa-Museo Lope de Vega, has been opened to the public around the corner on Calle Cervantes (walk down Calle Léon and then take a left). Lope de Vega (1562-1635) was one of the most prolific and charismatic writers of Madrid's Golden Age. He churned out thousands of plays, poems and satires, poked fun at all his rivals (especially Cervantes) and still found time to lead a stormy love life which scandalized and enthralled Spanish society. Vega bought this house in 1610 and lived here until his death in 1635; he loved his new home ('my little house, my tranquillity, my little plot, my study' he wrote not long after moving in) and it is now a delightfully intimate and serene museum. At the back is a peaceful, enclosed garden which was Vega's pride and joy and has been beautifully restored to look much as it would have when he would sit here and read five centuries ago (the staff are happy to let visitors do the same now).

Vega fared better than his arch-rival Cervantes, whose former home – just up the street at the corner of Calles Léon and Cervantes – was demolished in the early 19th century despite a loud chorus of public outrage. The site is now marked with a plaque.

Calle Huertas and Calle Atocha

On the corner of Calle Léon and Calle Huertas is the **Real Academia de la Historia** ① *C/Léon 21, T914 290 611, open by appointment to researchers*, which is housed in an imposing, if dour, 18th-century building by Juan de Herrera, originally designed as a shop for the monks of El Escorial who wanted a place to flog their rosary beads and bibles. **Calle Huertas** was once known as the street with 'more whores than doors', but now the brothels have made way for bars, restaurants, and jazz cafés. Beyond the main entertainment strip is the forbidding, walled complex of the **Convento de las Trinitarias Descalzas** (not open to visitors), which was founded in 1612, and once housed the daughters of Lope de Vega and Cervantes who both became nuns. Cervantes was buried here, but, in inimitable Madrileño fashion, his bones – like the bones of most of the city's most celebrated citizens – have been lost. A memorial Mass is still held here on the anniversary of his death.

Calle Atocha runs more or less parallel with Calle Huertas: noisy, slightly seedy and lined with cheaper *pensiones* and *hostales,* it's one of the main arteries of central Madrid. Just off Plaza Antón Martín at the top of the street is Madrid's most delightful cinema, the Art Deco **Cine Doré** which is now the **Filmoteca Nacional** (see page 67). It has a very pretty café and terrace, too.

Carrera de San Jerónimo

The Carrera de San Jerónimo leads down from the Puerta de Sol to the Cortes (Parliament), and is lined with showy banks and fancy offices. It's a dull street, but worth a visit to pick up some *túrron* (nougat) at the **Casa Mira** at No 31 or peek in at the most famous gourmet institution in all Madrid: **Lhardy** at No 8, where you can still help yourself to consommé from a silver samovar or dine upstairs in the panelled dining rooms where the nymphomaniac Queen Isabel II used to entertain her lovers.

Congreso de los Diputados

ⓘ *Plaza de las Cortes, C/San Jeronimo, T913 906 525, www.congreso.es. Metro Banco de España or Sevilla. Guided tours here have been suspended while restoration work takes place. See the website for up-to-date information.*

Continuing down the Carrera de San Jerónimo, you could easily walk past Spain's **Cortes** (Parliament) and dismiss it as another boring bank. It's a dreary greyish neo-building guarded by a pair of bronze lions. Inside, things liven up and it looks much more suited for the serious business of governing the country, with plenty of 19th-century plush red velvet, stained glass, and enormous chandeliers. Back in 1981, Spain's fledgling democracy came under threat when Colonel Tejero and his troops stormed the main assembly hall, firing off shots (the bullet holes can still be seen, but you have to ask discreetly), and took the Cortes (parliament) hostage for more than 24 hours. The nation, listening to the drama on the radio, held its breath, but democracy finally won out when leaders of all political parties banded together in a mass demonstration through the streets of Madrid.

Around the Cortes

Opposite the Parliament is the **Hotel Palacios**, a big cream cake of a hotel with liveried footmen and enormous chandeliers. The Calle del Duque de Medinaceli next to it leads to an ugly modern church, the **Iglésia Jesús de Medinaceli**, built to house a much-revered 16th-century statue of Jesús de Medinaceli. According to legend, the statue was stolen by pirates who demanded its weight in gold as ransom. But when the exchange took place and the statue was placed on the scales, it was miraculously found to weigh only as much as a single coin. On the first Friday of each month, queues snake endlessly around the church, waiting patiently to touch the statue and beg for miracles. Just across the small square outside the church is one of Madrid's most emblematic tiled bars, the **Taberna Dolores**.

Prado and Triángulo del Arte

Three of Europe's most important art museums – the Prado, the Thyssen-Bornemisza and the Reina Sofía – are all happily nudged up within strolling distance of each other (although only the most fanatical art-buff would consider visiting all three in a single day). Each of the three corners of the so-called 'Triángulo del Arte' has a particular strength: the Prado is famous for its magnificent collection of Spanish masterpieces from the 12th to the 19th centuries including works by Velázquez, Zurbarán and Goya; the luminous Reina Sofía continues the thread, displaying works spanning the last 150 years or so, including Picasso's celebrated Guernica; and the Thyssen-Bornemisza perfectly complements both collections, plugging the gaps left by the Prado with its vast collection of western European art spanning eight centuries, and offering a dazzling selection of early 20th-century masters from Braque to Kandinsky to whet your

Highlights of Paseo del Arte

Prado
Ground floor
Murals from the Hermitage of Santa Cruz de Maderuelo; *Self-Portrait*, Albrecht Dürer; *Annunciation*, Fra Angelico; *Descent from the Cross*, Roger van der Weyden; *The Triumph of Death*, Breughel the Elder; *The Garden of Delights*, Bosch; *Annunciation*, El Greco; Titian portraits.

First floor *Artemisia*, Rembrandt; Velázquez's masterpieces, especially *Las Meninas* and *The Surrender of Breda*; *Santa Isabel de Portugal*, Zurbarán; *The Three Graces*, Rubens; *El Martirio de San Felipe*, Ribera; *El Tres de Mayo*, Goya; Goya's *Pinturas Negras*.

Second floor *The Nude Maja* and *The Clothed Maja*, Goya.

Thyssen-Bornemisza
Ground floor *The Staircase* (second state), Leger; *New York City, New York*, Mondrian; *Harlequin with a Mirror*, Picasso; *Reclining House*, Klee; *Catalan Peasant with a Guitar*, Miró; *Green on Maroon*, Rothko; *Brown and Silver I*, Pollock; *Hotel Room*, Hopper; *Last Portrait*, Freud; *Woman in a Bath*, Lichtenstein.

First floor *Family Group*, Hals; *Pierrot Content*, Watteau; *Asensio Julià*, Goya; *Portrait of a Farmer*, Cézanne; *Houses Next to the River*, Shiele; *Quappi in a Pink Sweater*, Beckmann.

Second floor *Annunciation Diptych*, Van Eyck; *Madonna and Child Enthroned*, Van de Weyden; *Portrait of Giovanna Tornabuoni*, Ghirlandaio; *Portrait of Henry VIII*, Holbein; *Jesus Among the Doctors*, Dürer; *Annunciation*, El Greco; *The Garden of Eden*, Jan Breughel I; *The Toilet of Venus*, Rubens.

Reina Sofía
Second floor *The Gathering at the Café del Pombo*, Solana; *The Singer*, Gris; *Great Prophet*, Gargallo; *Guernica*, Picasso; *Constellation*, Calder; *Portrait of Joella*, Dalí and Man Ray; *Woman*, Miró.

Fourth floor *Homage to Mallarmé*, Oteiza; *Reclining Figure*, Bacon; *Spatial Concept, Hope*, Fontano; *Man and Woman*, Lupez; *Seven Chairs*, Tàpies; *Buen Retiro Ducks*, Schnabel; *The Spirit of the Birds*, Chillida.

---

appetite for the Reina Sofía. There are a smattering of smaller museums in the quiet streets behind the Prado, and then there's the cool, green expanse of the Parque del Retiro to get lost in afterwards.

Museo del Prado
ⓘ *Paseo del Prado s/n, T913 302 800 (tickets T902 107 077), www.museodelprado.es, Metro Banco de España. Mon-Sat1000-2000, Sun 1000-1900, closed 1 Jan, Good Friday, 1 May and 25 Dec. €12/€16. Free Mon-Sat 1800-2000, Sun 1700-1900. The sheer scale can make it daunting; it is wise to pick out some highlights or favourite painters and make a beeline for them before museum fever sets in. Note that the collection is regularly moved; pick up a plan at the entrance.* The Prado houses one of the world's greatest art collections, a dazzling display of European art spanning seven centuries. When it opened in 1819, it was one of the very

first public art museums, infused with the spirit of the Enlightenment, and shored up by royal whim (the Queen had been impressed with the Louvre and wanted one for Spain). The collection is enormous; today, it holds several thousand works of art and has long outgrown Juan de Villanueva's severely elegant neoclassical building. Plans are afoot for a major expansion by architect Rafael Moneo which is scheduled for completion in 2005. The Casón del Buen Retiro, which holds the museum's collection of 19th-century art, is currently closed indefinitely for reconstruction.

Carlos I began the royal collection, his son Felipe II expanded it, but it was Felipe IV who turned it into the most important art collection of his age. It still reflects the idiosyncratic tastes of the kings and queens who formed it, and is uneven in parts – some major Spanish artists like Ribera or Murillo are barely featured, for example.

Ground floor The ground floor holds the earliest works in the Prado's collection. The collection of medieval art is thin but includes some gilded retablos, and the haunting murals from the Hermitage of Santa Cruz de Maderuelo. Among the works from 15th-16th century Flanders are Van der Weyden's moving masterpiece, the *Descent from the Cross*, some sharply observed portraits by court painter Antonio Muro (originally from Utrecht), and the crowd-pleasing, nightmarish visions of Breughel the Elder and Bosch. There isn't much from the Italian Renaissance, but what there is is exquisite: Fra Angelico's *Annunciation*, Raphael's *Fall on the Road to Calvary*, and a series of beautiful panels by Botticelli depicting a story from the Decameron. Dürer's self-portrait is the highlight of the collection of 15th- and 16th-century German art, but don't miss the luminous panels depicting *Adam and Eve*. El Greco's paintings, with their dazzling colours, and surging, elongated forms, are given a room of their own (fans should visit Toledo, see page 91) and Titian, a favourite with Carlos I (Charles V) and Felipe II, is extremely well represented, along with his fellow Venetian painters, Veronese and Tintoretto. This floor also contains the museum's collection of classical sculpture.

First floor ⓘ *This is where the cream of the Prado's collection is held and where the crowds are inevitably thickest.* The excellent collection of French, Dutch and Italian paintings from the 17th and 18th centuries may be the envy of art museums around the world, but they are still completely overshadowed by the Prado's greatest treasure, its huge collection of works by Diego Velázquez (1599-1660), court painter to Philip IV. The most famous paintings are gathered under the glass dome at the very centre of the building, including *Las Meninas*, the subtle, sublime portrait of the Infanta Margarita and her maids-in-waiting, and an acutely observed portrait of *Felipe IV* himself. The celebrated painting of *The Surrender of Breda*, and the equestrian portraits painted for the Salon de los Reinos (in the present Army Museum) may one day be returned to their original setting (see below). There are some stark, brilliantly lit paintings by Zurbarán, a handful of fluffy saints by Murillo, and some dark, intense depictions of martyrs by José de Ribero. Rubens is well represented, because the Flemish painter was in the service of the Habsburg court, and visited Madrid several times. Finally, there are a series of rooms devoted to Franciso Goya y Lucientes (1746-1828), court painter to Carlos IV. On this floor you'll find the grim works painted after the anti-French uprisings of 1808 (see page 53), and the horrifying Black Paintings (*Pinturas Negras*), dark, hallucinatory pieces which were painted after the strange illness which left him deaf. (If you want to keep things strictly in chronological order, head upstairs to see his earlier, lighter paintings and leave the *Pinturas Negras* until last).

Second floor A whole wing of this floor is devoted to **Goya**. Before war and sickness plunged Goya into depression, his works were characterized by joyful scenes and vivid colours. The early tapestry cartoons sparkle with life, but Goya's most famous works are the mysterious *Clothed* and *Nude Maja*, daringly modelled, some say, on Goya's beautiful, and unconventional patron, the Duchess of Alba.

Basement Down in the basement, you'll find the **Dauphin's Treasure**, a dazzling collection of jewelled Renaissance and Baroque tableware and glassware, which originally belonged to Louis de Bourbon, son of Louis XIV. It's one of the most remarkable collections of its kind in the world; a single goblet is encrusted with 23 emeralds, plus plenty of cameos and cornelians. The café-restaurant is also tucked away down here, too – but there's not a jewel-encrusted salt cellar in sight.

Museo Thyssen-Bornemisza

① *Paseo del Prado 8, T902 760 511, www.museothyssen.org, Metro Banco de España, Mon 1200-1600, Tue-Sun 1000-1900, closed 1 Jan, 1 May and 25 Dec, €9/€6 concessions, free on Mon.*

The Museo Thyssen-Bornemisza is housed in an elegant palace just across the road from the Prado. When the Thyssen-Bornemisza collection was bought by the Spanish state in 1993, it proved an uncannily neat complement to the works held in the Prado and the Reina Sofía. It fleshes out the collections of medieval Flemish and Italian art held at the Prado, and adds an international dimension to the 20th-century art at the Reina Sofía. The museum collection is supplemented by the Collección Carmen Thyssen-Bornemisza, currently arranged in the adjoining (and interconnected) building. While this collection is not quite as impressive as the main collection, it nonetheless boasts some very fine pieces, notably works from the 17th and 18th centuries.

Second floor The visit begins on the second floor with the Thyssen's exceptional collection of medieval art. It opens with the luminous works of the Italian Primitives, followed by some glittering, highly decorative paintings in the International Gothic style which swept across Europe in the early 15th century. Van der Weyden, Van Eyck and Campen are among the early Dutch and Flemish masters, and there are some beautiful Renaissance portraits, including Holbein's celebrated portrait of Henry VIII. Moving into the 17th and 18th centuries, the bold energy of the Venetian colourists – there are stunning works by Titian, Veronese and Tintoretto – is echoed in El Greco's swirling, vibrant paintings, and there's a gaudy selection of sentimental 17th-century Baroque art from England, Flanders and Italy. There are several fleshy pieces by Rubens, hung beside Breughel's glowing *Garden of Eden*, and Bruggen's compelling depiction of *Esau Selling his Birthright*.

First floor Downstairs on the first floor, there are dozens of examples of Dutch genre painting – a bit on the dull side at first, but strangely absorbing when you look at them more closely. Architecture, everyday objects and landscapes were becoming increasingly important, and would pave the way for the Golden Age of Dutch art a few decades later. Two galleries are devoted to 19th-century North American art, rarely seen in European museums, including some beautiful light-drenched pieces by John Singer Sargent. There are a couple of late Goyas, some wistful, bucolic scenes by Corot, and a small collection of Impressionist and post-Impressionist works which include Degas' delightful *Swaying Dancer*, a couple of swirling Van Gogh's, and Cézanne's richly textured *Portrait of a Farmer*. A gallery is devoted to the dazzling colours of the Fauvists, but the highlight is the collection of Expressionist painting, with works by Schiele, Munch, Kandinsky, Macke, Otto Dix and Max Beckmann.

Ground floor On the ground floor, the blazing colours and wheeling forms of the experimental artists of the early 20th century seem to leap from the walls: Picasso's splintered *Man with a Clarinet*, Léger's weaving *The Staircase (second state)*, or Mondrian's obsessively geometric *New York City, New York*. These galleries are a roll-call of the biggest names in 20th-century art – Picasso, Miró, Kandinsky, Pollock, Rothko, Dalí are just some of the artists featured. Lichtenstein's knowing cartoonish *Woman in a Bath*, and a distorted portrait by Francis Bacon are among the most recent works.

The Collección Carmen Thyssen-Bornemisza, amassed by Carmen Cervera, former Miss Spain and fifth wife of Baron Hans Heinrich Thyssen-Bornemisza, is currently arranged in galleries which adjoin those containing the main collection. There are about 200 pieces in the collection, and highlights include works by Canaletto, Fragonard, Monet, Renoir and Picasso.

Museo Nacional Centro de Arte Reina Sofía

ⓘ *C/Santa Isabel 52, T914 675 062, www.museoreinasofia.mcu.es, Metro Atocha. Mon, Wed-Sat 1000-2100, Sun 1000-1430, €6/€3 concessions (Abono Paseo del Arte €21.60, includes entrance to the Prado and Thyssen-Bornemisza museums), free Sat afternoon and Sun, and Mon, Wed, Fri 1900-2100. Giftshop and café.*

The third corner of the Triangulo del Arte is tucked away at the bottom of the Calle Atocha, a 10-minute walk away from the Prado. It's housed in a former hospital, which has been beautifully remodelled to hold the nation's collection of 20th-century art. It's a graceful, light-filled building set around a quiet, interior courtyard, with a pair of panoramic glass lifts which are almost an attraction in themselves. The second and fourth floors are devoted to the permanent exhibition, and the first and third floors are used for temporary exhibitions which are usually excellent. Jean Nouvel's 2004 extension, a curving glassy building, houses the excellent café-restaurant and library.

Second floor The artworks on the second floor trace the development of Spanish art from the turn of the twentieth century to the conclusion of the Civil War in 1939. José Solana's *The Gathering at the Café del Pombo* reflects the intensity of intellectual life in Madrid's cafés, but it was the Basques and the Catalans who were creating the most innovative work in painting and sculpture; Isidre Nonell's haunting studies of gypsies in the streets of Barcelona profoundly influenced Picasso's Blue period. At the start of the 20th century, Paris was the mecca of the art world, and Spanish artists soaked up the Avant Garde art movements; Juan Gris developed his personal interpretation of Cubism, and Pau Gargallo's whiplash, wrought-iron sculptures treated space in an entirely new way. Both collaborated with Picasso, whose works are displayed in a line of galleries here.

At the centre is *Guernica*, his vast, anguished response to the bombing of a Basque village during the Civil War. The Picasso galleries are flanked by a succession of galleries devoted to Joan Miró, who created a personal sign language in his colourful, abstract paintings. There are some light, graceful mobile sculptures by Calder, and two rooms are devoted to Dalí's surreal, melting landscapes. Finally, there's a mixed collection of sculpture, including pieces by Miró, and a lissom, suspended piece by Àngel Ferrant.

Fourth floor You can glide up in a glass lift to the fourth floor for post-war art. Spain's artistic and cultural life was mercilessly repressed in the first years of the Franco's dictatorship. During the 1950s, some of the most interesting work was being done by the Basque sculptor Jorge Oteiza, whose boxy, iron pieces inspired Equipo 57, a collective committed to exploring notions of space. There is a good collection of international artists – paintings by Francis Bacon, Yves Klein's trademark brilliant blue works, a tiny, serene sculpture by Henry Moore, and slashed canvases by Lucio Fontana. Several galleries are devoted to the late Catalan artist Antoni Tàpies, whose unsettling 'material paintings' are created from layers of 'found' objects. Antonio Lupez's vast sculpture *Man and Woman* is set alongside some haunting landscapes of Madrid. The Spanish collective Equipo Crónico attacked mass culture imported from the US in their Pop Art-style pieces from the late 1960s and 1970s, and the most recent works include a group of severely abstract sculptures from Eduardo Chillida.

Around the Prado

Paseo del Prado

The tree-lined Paseo del Prado sweeps between the Prado and the Thyssen-Bornemisza and connects two of Madrid's best-known monuments – at least to football fans. At the top of the Paseo is the **Plaza de Cibeles**, with flood-lit fountains and an enormous statue of the goddess **Cibeles** in her chariot at its centre. Real Madrid fans launch themselves at Cibeles to celebrate victories – she lost a hand in 1994 which had to be stuck back on with a special glue, and now she gets boarded up when danger looms. Just a few hundred metres away, at the other end of the Paseo del Prado, **Neptune** and his sea horses rear out of another fountain stuck in the middle of the Atocha roundabout. Neptune gets the Atlético fans, who also now face barricades on victory nights. Behind the Cibeles Fountains, you can't miss the soaring towers and extravagant neo-Gothic façade of what is now the city hall, but was, until very recently, the city's main post office. It still bears its handsome, century-old brass letter boxes and is called the **Palacio de las Comunicaciones**.

Casón del Buen Retiro (Centro de Estudios del Prado)

The hushed, elegant neighbourhood around the Prado is studded with smaller museums devoted to an eccentric range of special interests from pottery to plants. The Prado's annexe, Casón del Buen Retiro, is one of just two surviving buildings of the Royal Palace of the Buen Retiro which once stretched out across this whole eastern flank of the city.

Miraculously, the building has preserved one of the grandest ceremonial halls of the former palace, the dazzling Salón de los Reinos, blazing with the escutcheons of the 24 kingdoms which made up pain in the 17th century. Zurbarán was commissioned to paint a series of 10 canvases depicting the Labours of Hercules to adorn the hall, along with Velázquez's *The Surrender of Breda*, and several equestrian portraits of the royal family.

They are all currently on display at the Prado, and the Casón del Buen Retiro is the Prado's library and documentation centre.

CaixaForum

The **CaixaForum** ① *Paseo del Prado 36, T913 307 399, www.lacaixa.es/obrasocial, closed Mon, admission varies*, occupies a strikingly restored 19th-century power station right on the Paseo del Prado, which is crowned by a bold, rusted iron sculpture. A private cultural institution funded by a Spanish savings bank, it hosts excellent – and usually free – exhibitions, and has a great programme of workshops, talks, and family-friendly activities. By the main entrance, you can't miss the spectacular 'Vertical Garden' by renowned landscape artist Patrick Blanc.

Museo Naval

① *Paseo del Prado 5, T952 387 789, Tue-Sun 1000-1900, free, ID required.*
There's more on the military theme at the Museo Naval (Navy Museum), tucked away in the brutally ugly Ministry of Defence building a short stroll up the Paseo del Prado. The sections which deal with the Age of Discovery, when Spain ruled the seas and a great swathe of the known world, are fascinating, with maps and models showing how the 15th- and 16th-century explorers staked their claims to the New World.

Museo Nacional des Artes Decoratives

① *C/Montalbán 12, T915 326 499, http://mnartesdecorativas.mcu.es, Metro Banco de España, Tue-Fri 0930-1500, Sat-Sun, public holidays 1000-1400, €3/€1.50, free to over-65s, Sun.*
At the other end of the spectrum, just around the corner on Calle Montalbán, there's the National Museum of Decorative Arts, stuffed with furniture, porcelain, tapestries and tiles from all over Spain. Highlights include a pair of winsome Hansom cabs from the 17th-century, an elaborately tiled 18th-century Valencian kitchen, and a delightful collection of 19th-century dolls houses, complete with gilded wall paper and chandeliers. Several galleries are devoted to ceramics and porcelain, including the shimmering platters and vases typical of Manises.

Real Jardín Botánico

① *Plaza de Murillo 2, T914 203 017, www.rjb.csic.es, Metro Atocha, 1000-dusk daily, €3/€1.50.*
When museum fatigue sets in, head for the languid Real Jardín Botánico, which sits next to the southern entrance to the Prado on Plaza Murillo, and is cross-crossed with leafy paths and sprinkled with fountains. Established in the 16th century and given this elegant new home in the 18th century, there are now more than 30,000 plants on display including the Madrone or Strawberry Tree which has become the city's symbol.

Parque del Retiro

① *Entrances on C/Alfonso XII, C/Alcala, and Av Menéndez Pelayo. Daily 1000-dusk, free. Observatorio Nacional T915 061 261, www.ign.es/rom, visits by appointment, €5.*
Madrid likes to boast is that it is the greenest city in Europe, and one of its largest and loveliest parks extends for several hundred breezy acres behind the Prado. This dreamy expanse of manicured gardens, lakes, shady woods and pavilions once surrounded the

royal palace of the Buen Retiro and were handed over to the public in the 19th century. They've been enjoyed ever since, and the sandy paths are crammed on Sundays with families enjoying a stroll, or sitting at a lake-side café to enjoy the breeze.

The main entrance is next to the **Puerta de Alcalá**, a huge, triumphal arch topped with monstrous cherubs which was built in 1778 for no particular reason, and which has, inexplicably, become one of the city's favourite symbols. A sandy avenue leads to the Retiro's centrepiece, a stately *estanque* (lake) surrounded by columns and overlooked by a ridiculous statue of Alfonso XII. The lake used to be the scene of royal regattas, when galleons would set sail in mock-battles performed to entertain the court, but the closest you'll get nowadays is to hire a rowboat. This is the busiest section of the park, packed with buskers, fortune tellers, poets and tango dancers but you can easily find a quiet spot among the trees for a snooze or a picnic.

Just south of the lake are two beautiful pavilions, the **Palacio de Velázquez** and the ethereal **Palacio de Cristal**, now used by the Reina Sofía (see above) for temporary contemporary art exhibitions. At the southern end of the park, take a peek at the bizarre **Angel Caído** (Fallen Angel), one of only three monuments in the world to Satan, caught mid-way in his fall from Paradise.

Just by the southern entrance to the park, Juan de Villanueva's charming neoclassical **observatory** sits on a little hill overlooking the Retiro, and houses a dusty collection of old telescopes, sundials and sextants. Just beyond the park exit here is the Calle (usually called Cuesto) Claudio Moyano (heading downhill to Atocha train station), which is lined with a pretty row of wooden stalls piled high with second-hand books.

Estación Atocha
The area around Madrid's train station in the south of the city is as banal as most city suburbs, with its dull blocks of flats and busy main roads. But there are a few unusual sights tucked away in its depths, from freakishly tall skeletons to tropical gardens. The **tropical garden**, perhaps unexpectedly, is hidden inside Atocha train station. When the station was massively expanded in 1992 for the high-speed AVE trains to Seville, the original station with its graceful 19th-century wrought-iron and glass frame was converted into a hazy oasis complete with lofty palm trees and terrapins – perfect for a coffee on a wintry day. The big roundabout outside the station is home to a **statue of Neptune**, see page 45, overlooked by a very fanciful 19th-century building topped with fabulous creatures which looks like it should be something more exciting than the Ministry of Agriculture but isn't. Next to the station is a **memorial** to the 191 victims of the 2004 train bombings.

Museo del Ferrocarril and around
On the other side of Atocha train station is the charming **Museo Del Ferrocarril** (National Train Museum) ① *Paseo de las Delicias 61, www.museodelferrocarril.org, Tue-Sun 1000-1500, €5.09/€3.56,* where a vast collection of steam engines and model railways are held in a 19th-century train station with a wrought-iron canopy. Next to it is the entirely missable **Museo de la Ciencia y Tecnología** (Museum of Science and Technology) ① *www.muncyt.es, Tue-Sat 1000-1400 and 1600-1800, Sun 1000-1430, free,* which the interactive revolution seems to have passed by. You'll find more-up-to date attractions in the large, modern **Parque de Enrique Tierno Galván** (a 10-minute walk south) which has a **Planetarium** and an **IMAX** cinema.

Museo Antropología
ⓘ *C/Alfonso XII 68, Metro Atocha, Tue-Sat 1000-1930, Sun 1000-1400, €3/€1.50.*
Opposite the Neptune statue is the Anthropology Museum, a dusty old-fashioned museum with a rag-bag assortment of artefacts gathered from around the world. The nucleus of the collection was gathered by the eccentric Dr Pedro González Velasco, who famously embalmed his daughter and could be seeing driving around in his carriage with her body propped up beside him. A small room off the ground floor galleries contains the bizarre corpse of an extremely tall man – 2.35 m – who sold his body to science before his death.

Panteón des Hombres Ilustres
ⓘ *C/Julien Gayarre, Metro Menéndez Pelayo/Atocha. Apr-Sep Tue-Fri 0900-1900, Sat-Sun 0900-1600, Oct-Mar Tue-Fri 0930-1800, Sat-Sun 0900-1500, free.*
Head down the big, noisy Avenida de la Ciudad which flanks the train station to find more old bones in the Pantheon of Illustrious Men. Madrileños have lost the bones of most of their famous inhabitants from Cervantes to Velázquez and erected this Moorish-style pantheon in the 19th century in an attempt to rectify this habit – the names of its current inmates have long faded from memory.

Real Fábrica de Tapices
ⓘ *C/Fuentarrabía 2, T914 340 550, www.realfabricadetapices.com, Metro Menéndez Pelayo, Mon-Fri 1000-1400, guided visits only, €5.*
Almost opposite the Pantheon, with a discrete entrance on Calle Fuentarrabía, is the Royal Tapestry Factory, where tapestries have been woven for Spain's draughty royal palaces for several hundred years. You can watch the vast hangings being threaded by hand on enormous 18th-century wooden looms, a fascinating glimpse of a dying art.

La Latina and Lavapiés

The traditionally working-class neighbourhoods of La Latina and Lavapiés spread steeply downhill south of the Plaza Mayor. Known as *los barrios bajos* ('low neighbourhoods') as much for their position on the social ladder as their geographical location, they have traditionally been home to Madrid's poorest workers, smelliest industries, and most desperate immigrants. The latest wave of immigrants are more likely to be from North Africa or Latin America than Andalucía or Galicia, and the sinuous sounds of Arabic pop songs or Dominican salsa tunes regularly float above the rooftops. La Latina and Lavapiés are rapidly becoming Madrid's most multicultural neighbourhoods, and young artists are also moving in to add to the mix, bringing trendy bars, cafés and vintage clothes stores in their wake. The Sunday morning flea market **El Rastro** is a classic: follow it in true Madrileño style with a tapas crawl around the local bars.

La Latina
Plaza de la Paja and around The heart of La Latina is the Plaza de la Paja. This was once the most important square of medieval Madrid, but, until recently, it was sadly neglected. Newly spruced up, it has become one of the prettiest in Madrid, and the best example of the neighbourhood's continuing regeneration. Some of Madrid's hippest bars have opened their designer doors around the square and, on summer evenings, it teems with Madrid's

Being Madrileño

Few Madrileños can boast four Madrileño grandparents. Like most capital cities, it's a big melting pot for people from all over the country as well as a liberal sprinkling of immigrants from further afield. But being Madrileño is still a matter of pride, wherever your family once came from.

The *barrios bajos* are traditionally the most *castizo*, which literally means simply 'from Castile', but has come to mean authentically Madrileño. The inhabitants used to be known as 'Manolos' or 'Manolas', so called because the converted Jews who once lived here commonly named their eldest son 'Manolo'. They were known for their sharp tongues and their sharp dress sense; the men rejected French fashions for the classic Spanish cape, and the women famously tucked daggers in their stockings. Generations of travellers trawled the streets hoping for a glimpse of these romantic characters, but they had all but died out by the 19th century. Goya's Majos and Majas – similar in dress and attitude to the Manolos – live on in his cheerful depictions of 18th-century pilgrimages and festivals.

fashionable youth. Cut off from traffic, and scattered with a few trees and some benches, it is ringed with restored 19th-century palaces and overlooked by the handsome **Iglesia de San Andrés** ⓘ *open for Mass only*. The boring interior was almost completely destroyed in the Civil War, but the adjoining **Capilla del Obispo** (Bishop's Chapel) is a Renaissance gem, finally open for limited viewing after decades of restoration work.

The Plaza de la Paja is linked to the **Plaza de la Humilladero**, **Plaza de San Andrés** and **Plaza de los Moros**, which all form one large, pedestrian space on the other side of the San Andrés church. This is the place to come after the Rastro (see below), when everyone spills out of the surrounding tapas bars, kids run around with their footballs, and musicians play their bongos and guitars out in the sunshine. It's also the home of **Museu do los Orígenes (Casa San Isidro)** ⓘ *Plaza San Andrés 2, T913 667 415, Metro La Latina or Tirso de Molina, Tue-Fri 0930-2000 (until 1430 in Aug), Sat-Sun 1000-1400, free*. According to legend, San Isidro, patron saint of Madrid, and his equally saintly wife, Santa María de la Cabeza once lived here as servants to an aristocratic family. Countless miracles have been attributed to the saintly duo, but one of the most celebrated is the story of their drowned child, who fell down the well. The couple prayed and prayed and finally the well filled up and overflowed, disgorging their son, who was found to be perfectly fine. This very same well (honestly) has been incorporated into the building, along with the 17th-century Capilla de San Isidro, given a layer of Baroque frilliness in the 1790s, which is where the saint supposedly died. A section of the museum is devoted exclusively to the life and times of San Isidro and Santa María, another is devoted to the history of the city and features excellent temporary exhibitions, and there's also a garden which has examples of some of the trees to be found in medieval Madrid.

Catedral de San Isidro ⓘ *C/Toledo 37-39, T913 692310, Metro La Latina, Mon-Sat 0830-1230, 1830-2030, Sun and holidays 0900-1400, 1730-2030, free*. San Isidro's bones are kept in the Catedral de San Isidro, an enormous twin-towered Baroque church, was once the headquarters of the Jesuits in Madrid until their expulsion from Spain in 1767. The church was promptly altered to expunge all trace of the austere Jesuit style, the frothy

Churrigueresque façade was added, and it was rededicated to San Isidro who had been canonized in 1622. The remains of San Isidro and his wife were moved here from the church of San Andrés (to the fury of the local priest) and it served as the Madrileño cathedral until the Catedral de Nuestra Señora de la Almudena was completed in 1993.

Basílica de San Francisco el Grande ① *Plaza de San Francisco, T913 653 800, Metro La Latina, Tue-Sat 1100-1300, 1600-1830, €3.* Larger, grander and even gloomier than the Catedral de San Isidro, the Basílica de San Francisco el Grande (head west down Carretera de San Francisco from the Plaza Puerta de Moros) lives up to its name with a massive dome spanning more than 100 foot. It was built between 1762 and 1784 on the ruins of a hermitage supposedly founded by Saint Francis himself. It's in the middle of a lengthy restoration project and much of it is wrapped up in scaffolding and nets. Look out for Goya's early painting of San Bernadino de Siena in the chapel dedicated to the saint.

Puerta de Toledo and around This pompous gateway was erected in 1817 as a celebration of Ferdinand VI's return to the throne after Joseph Bonaparte's brief government. There are some excellent vintage clothes stores on Calle Mira el Rio Alta and Calle el Rio Baja just to the northeast. On Calle de la Paloma, you'll find the lovely neo-Mudéjar **Iglesia de la Virgen de la Paloma**, the focus of a delightful pilgrimage and festival in early August (see page 69).

Lavapiés
El Rastro ① *Metro Tirso de Molino or Puerta de Toledo.* Madrid's famous flea market takes place every Sunday morning. Stalls wind all the way up Calle Ribera de Curtidores and sell everything from tacky clothes and souvenirs to leather goods, underwear, arts and crafts, and kites. The street name means *Tanner's Alley* and recalls the pungent trades which took place down here out of sight (and smell) of the smart neighbourhoods at the top of the hill. 'Rastro' refers to the sticky trail of blood left when the meat carcasses were hauled through the streets. The neighbourhood is still a little shabby and run-down, although it's in the process of regeneration and half the streets seem to have been dug up, but the leather trade is now a thing of the past. The surrounding shops are mainly devoted to antiques and bric-a-brac, although you'll still find plenty of leather goods here too. Most shops are open all week, including Sunday mornings, but the days of a bargain are long gone. Watch out for your bags – the Rastro is notorious for pickpockets. The atmosphere is wonderful, and carries on long after the stall-holders have packed up, when everyone heads to the surrounding bars for some tapas and a well-earned cold beer.

Fábrica de Tabacos ① *C/de Embajadores, Metro Lavapiés.* At the height of its production, the enormous Royal Tobacco Factory employed 3000 women, the original Carmens, sharp-tongued beauties who were as famous for their solidarity as they were for their feistiness. They formed a powerful union and fought for an improvement in working conditions, including the establishment of schools, nurseries and pensions. By the early 20th century, mechanisation had taken its toll, and the once-grand factory now stands forlorn and empty. Plans to convert it into a museum have been stalled by the financial crisis.

Gran Vía, Chueca and Malasaña

The broad sweep of the Gran Vía was created at the dawn of a new age, wide enough for motor cars and lined with the city's first skyscrapers and cinemas (many of which preserve the old tradition of using handpainted billboards). Now a busy, traffic-clogged shopping street, it's looking a bit down-at-heel but it's brash, larger-than-life appeal still lingers. To the north of the Gran Vía are two formerly run-down neighbourhoods which have become the focal point of the city's heady nightlife: Chueca and Malasaña, which have both been dramatically cleaned up in the last decade. Chueca is the focal point of Madrid's gay community and Malasaña has a youthful, bohemian edge, but both are packed with some of the city's best cafés, most fashionable clubs, and trendiest shopping.

Parque del Oeste runs along the north west of the city: this is where the cable car leaves for the wild expanse of the **Casa del Campo** (with its zoo and funpark), and where you'll find the path to Goya's beautiful pantheon.

Gran Vía

Calle Alcalá Calle Alcalá is a swaggering introduction to the Gran Vía, with which it connects on the eastern side of the city. It's lined with flamboyant Belle Epoque buildings, like the glamorous Casino (members only, unless you can sweet-talk the doormen into giving you a glimpse of the billowing staircase), and the Art Deco **Circulo de Belles Artes** ⓘ *Metro Banco de España, Tue-Fri 1700-2100, Sat-Sun 1100-1400, café Mon-Thu, Sun 0900-1400, Fri-Sat 0900-0400*, now an excellent café-bar and cultural centre.

Plaza de la Lealtad The creamy curves of the Hotel Ritz overlook the circular garden of the Plaza de la Lealtad (Loyalty Square). The obelisk and eternal flame flickering in the middle of the garden commemorate the victims of the uprising on 2 May 1808, see page 53.

Real Academia de Bellas Artes de San Fernando ⓘ *C/Alcalá 13, T915 231 599, www.realacademiabellasartessanfernando.com, Tue-Sun 1000-1500, €5/€2.50*. The Royal Academy of Fine Arts has barely changed since Dalí was a student here in the 1920s – before he was expelled for questioning his professors' competence – and there's a lingering sense that the appreciation of art is a solemn business and any frivolity will be frowned on. Nonetheless, the Academy houses a rich and surprisingly extensive collection of paintings and drawings (many of which were appropriated after the Jesuits were expelled from Spain in 1767) including works by El Greco, Velázquez, Zurbarán, Ribera, Murillo, Veronese, Titian, Rubens, Fragonard, and Van Dyck. The Academy is most proud of its large collection of paintings by Goya, including several of his later works which are all imbued with an unsettling undercurrent: even the apparently innocent festival being celebrated in the *Burial of the Sardine* hints at something sinister in Goya's portrayal.

Torre Telefónica ⓘ *Gran Vía 28, entrance around the corner on C/Fuencarral 3, T915 226 645, Metro Gran Vía*. This was Spain's first skyscraper, a slick, 29-storey art deco construction which was built in 1929 to house an American telephone company. As the most instantly recognisable landmark in the city centre, it was targeted by Franco's forces during the Civil War, and kids used to collect the still-hot shrapnel embedded in its smooth façade. Spain's former national telephone company **Telefónica** own the building now, and have invested some of their billions in an exhibition space.

Plaza del Callao This circular square is filled with bus fumes and chaos but it's overlooked by one of the prettiest of the Gran Vía's art deco cinemas, the **Cinesa Capitol**, and the sleek **Palacio de la Prensa**, now also a cinema. The latter is one of the few which can still be counted on to erect a huge hand-painted advert for forthcoming attractions.

Plaza de España Plaza de España is a large, sandy square with a pair of huge ornamental fountains, and a couple of grassy areas usually colonized by picnicking office-workers and the odd tramp sleeping off a hangover. At the centre, Don Quixote and Sancho Panza sally forth on their next adventure, while Cervantes looks on gloomily. The square is overshadowed by a pair of bombastic skyscapers – the **Edificio de España** (1948) and the **Torre de Madrid** (1957).

 The delightful **Sabatini Gardens** (see page 37) and the **Templo de Debod** (see page 54) are a very short stroll from the Plaza de España – both much prettier places to sunbathe or picnic.

Museo Cerralbo ⓘ *C/Ventura Rodríguez 17, T915 473 646, http://museucerralbo.mcu.es, Metro Ventura Rodríguez, Tue-Sat 0930-1500, also Thu 1700-2000, Sun 1000-1500, €3/€1.50.* This beautiful 19th-century palace belonged to the 17th Marqués de Cerralbo, who crammed it with treasures picked up on his many travels. On his death in 1922, he bequeathed the palace and its contents to the state, with the stipulation that nothing was to be moved. As a result, it's delightfully, eccentrically cluttered, with Roman busts rubbing shoulders with Flemish tapestries, and paintings by Ribera, Murillo, and Zurbarán jostling up together in unfashionable proximity. The palace is fitted with breath-taking opulence; even the bathrooms are works of art, with pretty shell-shaped sinks and porcelain loos. The chandelier collection is extraordinary – don't miss the ultra-kitsch pink and blue one in the Music Room – but the highlight is the magnificent ballroom surrounded with huge gilded mirrors and festooned with garlands and swarms of cherubs.

Chueca
Plaza de Chueca Chueca is the heart of gay Madrid but it's also where most of the nightlife is concentrated. This square, with its terrace cafés and bars, may be quiet and nondescript by day, but livens up dramatically at night and is a great place to start the night.

Museo de Historia de Madrid ⓘ *C/Fuencarral 78, T917 011 863, Metro Tribunal, closed indefinitely for restoration; temporary exhibitions are held.* Madrid's town museum boasts one of the most extraordinary doorways in the city, a gushing Churrigueresque fantasy sculpted by Pedro de Ribera in the 17th century. Inside, there are plenty of plans and models, including Teixera's famous map made in 1656, a huge wooden model of early 19th-century Madrid, and some delightful models of the mock-battles which some used to take place on the Retiro lake (see page 46). There are furnishings, a huge collection of porcelain from the long-demolished Royal Factory of the Buen Retiro, and a series of otherwise indifferent paintings which are fascinating for the glimpses they give of the way

El Dos de Mayo

In early 1808, Napoleon's armies marched into Madrid with the co-operation of the cowardly Spanish king, Carlos IV. On May 2, a carriage containing the royal family slipped out of the palace gates. Unfortunately, a local locksmith saw them and immediately assumed that the Napoleonic armies were spiriting them away. A crowd gathered yelling "death to the French" and the city erupted into revolt.

There are dozens of tales of heroic deeds, but none more so than the seamstress Mañuela Malasaña, after whom this neighbourhood is named who was shot by the French soldiers after attacking them bravely with her scissors. Goya's celebrated works in the Prado – El Dos de Mayo 1808 and El Tres de Mayo 1808 – were painted six years later to immortalize the heroism of the Madrileños against the French troops.

Madrid used to look. Goya's famous *Allegory of Madrid* takes pride of place. When it was first painted (1810), the frame held by the female figure contained a portrait of Napoleon, but when the French were being beaten back a few years later, the offending portrait was painted over. Then Bonaparte came back into power and the painting had to be retouched – again. The uncertain political climate meant that the painting was eventually 'adjusted' seven times. Finally it was decided to paint it over with the words 2 de Mayo (Second of May) as a reminder of the uprising against the French occupiers (see box above).

Museo del Romanticismo ⓘ *C/San Mateo 13, T914 481 045, Metro Chueca, Tue-Sat 0930-2030, Sun 1000-1500, €3/€1.50.* This elegant palace is crammed with folk art, period furniture and minor paintings by Zurbarán, Goya and Sorolla, but its most obvious association with the Romantic movement is the collection of memorabilia belonging to Mariano José de Larra. A brilliant satirist and Romantic whose weekly newspaper column took a pitiless view of Madrid society, Larra shot himself (with the pair of duelling pistols on display) at the age of 28 over an unhappy love affair. It has a charming tea room and a small gift shop.

Sociedad General de Autores ⓘ *C/Fernando VI 4, www.sgae.es, Metro Alonso Martínez.* It took a Catalan, Grases Riera, to built this voluptuous, Art Nouveau beauty in the middle of Madrid. The creamy undulations of the Palacio Longoria are now the property of the General Society of Authors, who might let you in to peek at the flowing staircase with its delicate floral ironwork and rainbow-coloured stained glass ceiling.

Malasaña and around

The **Plaza de Dos de Mayo** (Second of May Square) is named for the famous uprising against the French in 1808 (see box, above). It is the focal point of Malasaña's excellent nightlife, with plenty of terrace cafés, clubs and bars. It used to be the scene of a huge *botellón* every weekend, when a sea of teenagers would descend, clutching their plastic bottles of booze (hence the name). But Madrid has cracked down firmly on the *botellón*, and cleaners stand by with hoses to make sure that the kids don't come back. Just off the square is **Calle San Vicente Ferrer**, which is sprinkled with old tiled shopfronts (including a pharmacy with a memorable advert for a laxative). At night this street is crammed pierced navel to pierced navel with hip students and teenagers queuing for the endless line of bars.

Centro Cultural Conde Duque ① *Plaza Conde Duque 9-11, T914 800 401, www.esmadrid.com/condeduque, Metro Noviciado. Check website for opening hours and prices.* This cultural centre housed in an enormous 18th-century barracks is home to the city's large collection of contemporary art, and also contains a concert hall, a library and galleries for temporary exhibitions. Just to the north is the sunny **Plaza de Comendadoros**, with a handful of hip terrace cafés, a good place for a drink.

Parque del Oeste The cool, shady Parque del Oeste spreads along the western flank of the city just a few minutes stroll north of the Plaza de España and west of Malasaña. One of its most surprising sights is a 2000-year-old temple, the **Templo de Debod** ① *C/Ferraz s/n, T917 651 008, Metro Ventura Rodriguez, Apr-Sep Tue-Fri 1000-1400 and 1800-2000, Oct-Mar 0945-1345, 1615-1815*, a gift from the Egyptians, perched on a low hill and reflected in a still pond in the south of the park. The surrounding peaceful gardens are very popular on Sunday mornings, when the benches are filled with locals reading their newspapers.

Ermita de San Antonio de la Florida y Goya Pantheon ① *Glorieta de la Florida 5, T915 420 722, Metro Príncipe Pío, Tue-Sun 0930-2000, free.* You can walk downhill – along Calle Francisco y Jacinto Alcántara – towards a pedestrian bridge which crosses the train tracks and leads to the Museo Pantéon de Goya. Goya was commissioned to decorate a new hermitage sheltering a cult statue of St Antony of Padua in 1798. He worked rapidly, completing the frescoes in just 120 days and utterly transforming the simple chapel. In the cupola, St Antony raises a murdered man to life, in order to exonerate his own father who had been unjustly accused of the crime. Around him swirl Goya's famous '*angelitas*', the plump, rosy-cheeked '*majas*' of La Latina and Lavapiés who appear in his joyful paintings of local festivals – this time they have been transformed into angels. Goya's remains were brought here in 1919, and the chapel was closed for worship a decade later. The replica chapel directly opposite is used for services and is still the focus of a popular pilgrimage each year on 13 June.

Casa de Campo and the téléferico (cable car) Madrid's **téléferico** ① *www.tele ferico.org, hours vary, generally it operates weekends only in winter, daily the rest of the year, check website for exact times, €4 one way, €6 return*, sways giddily across the city and out to the vast **Casa de Campo** ① *Paseo Pintor Rosales s/n, T915 411 118, Metro Argüelles*, a huge and beautiful park full of shady walks and cycling paths. There's a lake at the centre (you can't miss the huge jet of water at the centre) with a few cafés and a lively trade in prostitution which doesn't seem to faze anyone. There's a park information centre close to the lake which can give you information on the special botanic walks and some of the plants and wildlife that you might encounter. Also in the park are Madrid's **zoo-aquarium** and **Parque de Atracciones** (theme park).

Museo de América ① *Av Reyes Católicos 6, T915 492 641, Metro Moncloa, Tue-Sat 0930-1830 (until 2030 May- Sep), Sun 1000-1500, €3/€1.50.* There's an excellent giftshop and café, and right opposite is the Faro de Madrid, a glassy observation tower. This handsome, red-brick Art Deco museum displays Spain's collection of booty from the Americas, and tries to explain what Spain was doing there in the first place. It's large, extremely well laid out, and there's plenty to amuse kids, from shrunken heads and mummies, to slide shows and special family events. The highlights include The Treasure of the Quimbayas, the most important collection of pre-Columbian gold in the world, and an extremely rare Mayan Codex (13th-16th centuries) which recounts the arrival of the Spanish.

Salamanca

It's easy to feel overwhelmed in this part of the city; the 19th-century entrepreneurs built their broad avenues and flashy palaces here, and the 20th-century wheeler-dealers added a string of high-tech skyscrapers along the brutal Paseo de la Castellana with its constantly whizzing traffic. Salamanca has been a rich neighbourhood since the Marqués de Salamanca urged all his aristocratic friends to buy into his new development on the northeastern fringe of the city at the end of the 19th century. They came in droves, happy to escape the insanitary medieval jumble of old Madrid for this elegant grid of broad avenues and well-equipped mansions complete with flush toilets.

The neighbourhood is still Madrid's smartest district, home to *los yuppís*, and their glossy offspring (*pijos* or *pijas*). Salamanca is definitely the place to come if you want to exercise your plastic; the streets – particularly Calles Serrano, Goya and Velázquez – are lined with designer boutiques, swanky bars and chic restaurants. The string of *terrazas* (bars and clubs with terraces) along the Paseo de la Castellana are still a fashionable spot to see and be seen, but if you choose to party here, make sure you can hold your own against the perfectly groomed locals.

Paseo de Recoletas

Palacio de Linares and Casa de América ① *Paseo Recoletos 2, T915 954 800, www.casamerica.es, Metro Banco de España, opening hours and prices vary according to the exhibitions.* A century ago, everyone who was anyone wanted a mansion along the aristocratic Paseo de Recoletos. This is one of the few survivors, an elegant palace set in handsome gardens which was built by the Marqués de Linares in the 1890s. According to urban myth, the palace is still haunted by the Marqués and his wife. The Marqués defied his family and married a commoner, only to discover that she was his half-sister. The unhappy couple were forced to divide the palace into two apartments and live separately until their deaths, and they still wail about their miserable fate on stormy nights. The Palace has been sympathetically converted into the Casa de América, a cultural centre which hosts temporary exhibitions, film events, lectures and concerts with a Latin American theme. It also has an excellent restaurant, **Cien Llaves**.

Palacio Marqués de Salamanca ① *Paseo Recoletos 10, not open to visitors.* This is the most flamboyant of the surviving palaces on the Paseo Recoletos, and was built for the Marquis de Salamanca – the entrepreneur behind the construction of the whole Salamanca district. An extravagant, larger-than-life character who made and lost three fortunes, he lived here with his remarkable art collection and Spain's first private bathroom until the loss of his final fortune forced him out to the suburbs where he died abruptly in 1883. Appropriately, it has been the headquarters of a Spanish bank for most of the last century.

Opposite the palace is the legendary **Café Gijón** (see page 64), one of the most famous literary cafés at the turn of the 20th century.

Biblioteca Nacional ① *Paseo Recoletos 20, T915 807 800, www.bne.es, Metro Serrano, Mon-Fri 0900-1400, Sun 0900-1400, free.* The largest and grandest building on the Paseo de Recoletos is the florid pompous National Library, built in the 19th century under Isabel II. It contains every book printed in Spain since 1712, plus a collection of illuminated manuscripts, drawings by Goya and Velázquez, and the first book of Castilian (Spanish) grammar. You'll find an engaging history of the library and its valuable collection in the adjoining museum.

Museo Arqueológico Nacional ① *C/Serrano 13, T915 777 912, http://man.mcu.es, Metro Serrano, closed for restoration, check website for information.* Madrid's enormous archaeological museum is the most comprehensive in Spain, with a vast collection spanning several millennia. It shares the same building as the Biblioteca Nacional (see above) but the entrance is around the back on Calle Serrano. Highlights include an excellent reproduction of the Altamira caves in Cantabria, discovered in 1879 but thought to have been painted around 8500 BC, in which bison, stags, and boars career across the walls with astonishing realism – one boar even scuttles by on several feet, obviously painted in order to create the illusion of rapid movement. The most important and most famous piece in the whole museum is the Dama de Elche, thought to have been sculpted around 500BC, a mysterious bust of a woman whose enigmatic expression almost outdoes the Mona Lisa. Very little is known about the Iberian culture which was wiped out when the Romans conquered the Iberian Peninsula, and the Lady of Elche has perplexed archaeologists since her discovery in 1897. The museum also houses a fine collection of Roman mosaics including a wonderful depiction of *Bacchus and His Train* from Zaragoza; a heavily jewelled collection of Visigothic crowns and crosses from Toledo; intricate Islamic art including a precious ivory casket which belong to Caliph Al-Hakam in the 10th century; and some stunning examples of Gothic *artesonado* ceilings from Seville and Toledo.

Paseo de la Castellana
Museo Lázaro Galdiano ① *C/Serrano 122, T915 616 084, www.flg.es, Metro Rúben Darío, Mon, Wed-Sat 1000-1630, Sun 1000-1500, €6/€3.*
Don José Lázaro Galdiano amassed one of the most extraordinary private art collections in Madrid, which he bequeathed to the state on his death in 1942. It is displayed in the very elegant surroundings of his Italianate home in a quiet leafy corner of Salamanca. The collection is astonishingly eclectic and includes archaeological artefacts, paintings, sculptures, armour, furniture, jewellery and one of the finest collections of enamels and ivories in existence. Among the paintings are works by Bosch, Rembrandt, Zurbarán, Velázquez, El Greco and Goya.

Museo Sorolla ① *C/General Martínez Camps 37, T913 101 584, http://museosorolla.mcu.es, Metro Rúben Darío, Tue-Sat 0930-2000, Sun and holidays 1000-1500, €3/€1.50 concessions, free on Sun.* This is one of Madrid's most delightful small museums, devoted to the Valenciano painter Joaquín Sorolla who lived here until his death in 1923. He enjoyed considerable success both internationally and among Madrid's new bourgeoisie at the end of the 19th century. His luminous paintings borrowed some of the techniques of French Impressionism, but his figures and landscapes are modelled with a sharp clarity. The upper galleries display his light-filled, happy paintings of children and pretty country scenes and seascapes while the lower floor has been left intact to give some insight into the artist's everyday life. Sunlight streams in from the huge skylights in his studio, and the living areas display his collection of popular jewellery, a mixed bag of ear-rings, religious medals and other odds and ends collected on his travels. The house stands in a tiny Moorish-style garden, deliciously cool in summer, with palms, tiles, fountains.

La Residencia de Estudiantes ⓘ *C/Pinar 23, T915 636 411, www.residencia.csic.es, Metro Gregorio Marañón, times and prices vary according to the exhibitions, closed Sat afternoon and Sun.* The Students' Residence (usually known simply as '*el resi*') was completed in 1915, and rapidly became one of the most influential and dynamic institutions in Spain. Famously, it was here that Lorca, Dalí and Buñuel met and became friends in the 1920s, developing their ground-breaking theories about art and literature. After the Civil War, the Residencia stultified under Franco's repressive regime. It now hosts some of the most stimulating temporary exhibitions in Madrid.

Fundación Juan March ⓘ *C/Castelló 77, T914 354 240, www.march.es, Mon-Sat 1100-2000, Sun and holidays 1000-1400, free.* This cultural centre was established by the Catalan tycoon Juan March in the 1950s (before he got banged up for cooking the books in the 1970s). It hosts excellent temporary exhibitions and major retrospectives and also offers a regular programme of music concerts.

Ventas

There's nothing to see out in the mainly residential neighbourhood of Ventas except Madrid's bullring. The 'Cathedral of Bullfighting', as it is often called, is the largest bullring in Spain, built in the 1930s, with capacity for 22,300 spectators. The **Bullfighting Museum** ⓘ *C/Alcalá 237, Plaza de las Ventas, Patio de Caballos, T917 251 857, www.las-ventas.com, Metro Ventas, Tue-Fri 0930-1430, Sun and bullfight days 1000-1300, free,* is at the back, near the horses' stables, with portraits of famous bullfighters, costumes, *banderillas* (the plumed daggers used to slow down the bull) and the stuffed heads of famous bulls. Most gruesome of all are the bloodstained clothes which belonged to some of the *toreros* who met their deaths in the bullring; one of the most recent was 'Yiyo' who died here in 1985, who is commemorated by a statue outside the ring. The first 'arm-to-arm' blood transfusion took place in the Plaza de Toros Monumental de las Ventas; celebrated bullfighter Manolete, died here in August 1947.

◉ Madrid listings

For Where to stay and Restaurant price codes and other relevant information, see pages 10-19.

🛏 Where to stay

There is plenty of choice in Madrid, whether you're looking for a family-run *pensión* or a swish 5-star hotel with all the luxury trimmings. As always, you'll find the best deals online. Chain hotels normally offer good weekend deals, and prices drop in August when many businesses close. Note that many smaller *hostales* and *pensiones* are closed in Aug, the traditional holiday month. Exterior rooms are usually sunnier and noisier, while interior rooms are stuffier but a bit quieter. Ear plugs are pretty much essential.

In general, most moderate to inexpensive accommodation is clustered in the nightlife areas around the Plaza de Santa Ana, or north of the Gran Vía in Chueca and Malasaña. Smart Salamanca has the upmarket business hotels and a few chi-chi little boutique hotels, and the area around the Plaza Mayor and the Royal Palace mainly offers traditional hotels in the moderate to expensive price range.

Old Madrid *p30, maps p28 and p32*
€€ Chic&Basic Mayerling, C/Conde de Ramanones 6, T914 201 580, www.chicandbasic.com. Affordable chic is the appeal at this hotel, where the designer rooms are compact but well equipped.
€€ Hostal Conchita, C/Preciados 33, T915 224 923, and **Hostal Conchita II**, C/Campomanes 10, T915 475 061, www.hostalconchitaii.com. Recently completely refurbished, both these *hostales* offer remarkably good value for money. Rooms are equipped with bathrooms and fridges, and are very centrally located. An excellent choice for budget travellers.
€€ Hotel Plaza Mayor, C/Atocha 3, T913 600 606, www.h-plazamayor.com. This charming hotel right next to the Plaza Mayor offers simple, pristine rooms. It's worth splashing out on the suite, which has a private terrace and romantic rooftop views.
€€ Room-Mate Mario, C/Campomanes 4, T915 488 548, www.room-matehotels.com. A far cry from the pseudo-rustic decor of most small hotels; this boasts ultra-slick decor throughout, charming staff, perfect central location, and a very reasonable price. A highly recommended option.
€ Hospedaje Madrid, C/Esparteros 6, T915 220 060, www.hospedajemadrid.com. East of the Plaza Mayor, this friendly, welcoming *hostal* offers modern, attractive rooms decorated with pine or wrought iron furniture. En suite bathrooms with hairdryers, a/c and TVs. Self-catering apartments are also available.

Plaza de Santa Ana and around *p38, maps p28 and p32*
€€€€ Hotel Palace, Plaza de las Cortes 7, T913 608 000, www.westinpalace madrid.com. Dripping with chandeliers and crawling with liveried footman, this sumptuous Belle Epoque-style hotel offers luxury on a grand scale. It's perfectly located for the visiting 3 big museums of the Paseo del Arte.
€€€€ Villa Real, Plaza de las Cortes 10, T914 203 767, www.derbyhotels.es. Chic boutique-style hotel, with large, ochre-painted rooms decorated with a stylish mix of antiques and modern art and sculpture. The excellent restaurant, **East 47**, serves superb tapas. There's also a sauna and gym. Suites are available with jacuzzis.
€€€ Tryp Ambassador, Cuesta de Santo Domingo 5, T902 144 440, www.melia.com. A chain, but set in the magnificent former palace of the Duques de Granada; many of the original fittings have been retained, although the well-equipped rooms are

blandly decorated in universal chain hotel style. Good-value packages are available online.

€€ Hostal Adria Santa Ana, C/Núñez de Arce 15, T91 521 1339, www.hostal adriano.com. Colourfully decorated guest rooms, friendly staff and extras like Wi-Fi and air-conditioning make this a great budget bet.

€€ Hostal Adriano, C/Cruz 26, T913 605 872, http://hostaladriano.com. Sunny rooms with cheerful, brightly painted walls and modern furnishings.

€€ Hostal Astoria, C/Carrera de San Jerónimo 30-32, T914 291 188, www.hostal-astoria.com. High up on the 5th floor of a lovely 19th-century building, this is a very comfortable *hostal* with attractive rooms decorated with light floral prints and en suite bathrooms with hairdryers.

€€ Hostal Cervantes, C/Cervantes 34, T914 298 365, www.hostal-cervantes.com. This *hostal* is a big favourite because the friendly owners have succeeded in making it feel like a home away from home. There's a cosy lounge, each room has been decorated with pretty blue prints and have en suites.

€€ Hostal Jaen, C/Cervantes 5, T914 294 858, www.hjaen.com. This hostel is a little plusher than the usual barebones style and the owners are extremely helpful. It's located on a quiet street and, best of all, it offers 3 apartments at very good rates (apartments from €60 per night).

€ Hostal Fonda Horizonte, C/Atocha 28, 2ºB, T913 690 996, www.hostalhorizonte.com. Run by a delightful brother and sister team, Julio and María-Begoña, this is a friendly little *hostal*, offering charming rooms with and without bathrooms.

Prado and Triangulo del Arte *p40, maps p28 and p32*
€€€ Hotel Husa Paseo del Arte, C/Atocha 123, T912 984 800, www.hotelhusapaseodel arte.com. This modern hotel enjoys a prime

location within a short stroll of all three of the top art museums (the Prado, the Thyssen and the Reina Sofía).

Gran Vía, Chueca and Malasaña *p51, maps p28 and p32*
€€€€ Hotel Ritz, Plaza de la Lealtad 5, Gran Vía, T917 016 767, www.ritz.es. Madrid's Grande Dame of the hotel world, this lavish, creamy confection has a wonderful setting right by the Prado. Pure luxury, with a fine restaurant and chic cocktail bar which was a favourite with Dalí. The leafy terrace with thickly cushioned wicker chairs is a delight in summer.

€€€ De Las Letras H&R, Gran Vía 11, T915 237 980, www.hoteldelasletras.com. Crisp modern guest rooms and suites dedicated to different authors in a beautifully restored century-old building on the Gran Vía. There's also a fashionable roof terrace and bar with amazing views.

€€€ Hotel Atlántico, Gran Vía 38, T915 226 480. This large hotel is set in a 19th-century mansion slap bang in the middle of the Gran Vía. Each room is individually decorated and staff are very attentive.

€€€ Hotel Emperador, Gran Via 53, T915 472 800, hemperador@sei.es. A very popular, centrally located hotel, which has slightly dated rooms, but is redeemed by its elegant original fittings and a stunning rooftop pool.

€€ Hostal Hispano Argentino, Gran Vía 15, 6th floor, T915 322 448. Stuffed with knick-knacks and plants, this cheerful *hostal* is located in a beautiful 19th-century building on the Gran Vía. Rooms have bright bed covers plenty of prints and dried flowers. Triples are also available.

€€ Hostal Lauria, Gran Vía 50, T915 419 182, www.hostal-lauria.com. Friendly staff and a great location – the views from the sitting room are amazing. The best rooms (all with bathrooms) face out and also have extraordinary views.

Salamanca *p55, map p28*

€€€€ Hotel Orfila, C/Orfila 6,
T917 027 770, www.hotelorfila.com.
Converted from a luxurious 19th-century
mansion, the **Hotel Orfila** offers discreet
5-star luxury (it's part of the prestigious **Relais**
and **Chateaux** group) and has just 28 rooms
and 4 suites, all decorated individually in a
modern take on 19th-century style. There's a
beautiful, flower-scented terrace, a charming
salon de té, and a renowned restaurant. One
of the most charming hotels in the city.

€€€€ Hotel Santo Mauro, C/Zurbano 36,
T913 196 900, www.ac-hoteles.com.
This is a favourite with visiting celebrities who
want to avoid the public gaze. Each room in
this charming 19th-century mansion has
been individually decorated, many in a slick
minimalist style. Beautiful public areas with
plump sofas and antique fireplaces, tree-filled
gardens and a large pool. There's a handsome
restaurant set in the former library.

Restaurants

Madrid, as you would expect from a major
European city, offers a huge choice of eateries
from Argentine steaks to Japanese sushi.
Reservations are essential for virtually every
restaurant featured, especially at weekends.
Madrileños eat breakfast on the run, usually a
milky coffee and a pastry at around 0730 or
0800. They might leave the office for a plate
of *churros* (strips of fried donut-like batter)
dipped in a thick hot chocolate at around
1000. Lunch is eaten late, usually around
1430, with perhaps some tapas after work at
around 1900 or 2000. Dinner is rarely eaten
before 2200.

Old Madrid *p30, maps p28 and p32*
Restaurants
€€€€ La Terraza del Casino, C/Alcalá,
T915 321 275. Celebrity chef Paco Roncero is
at the helm of this stunning restaurant which
serves some of the finest and most creative
cuisine in the city. Jaime Hayon designed the

gorgeous interior, but the highlight is still the
fabulous terrace.

€€€ Casa Botín, C/Cuchilleros 17,
T913 664 217, www.restaurantebotin.com,
Metro Sol. This rambling, stone-built
restaurant tucked into what was once
the city walls is the oldest restaurant in
Madrid (founded in 1725). It's touristy, but
it's still one of the best places to try the
Madrileño speciality of *cochinillo* – roast
suckling pig.

€€€ Casa Paco, Plaza Puerta Cerrada 11,
T913 663 166, Metro La Latina. Closed Sun
and Aug. A resolutely old-fashioned tiled bar
with a restaurant at the back. Dignified
waiters in long aprons serve traditional
sizzling grilled meats, accompanied by a
good selection of Spanish wines. Black and
white photographs show the founder posing
with everyone from Catherine Deneuve to
the King of Spain. Simple tapas are available
at the bar.

€€€ Cornucopia, C/Navas de Tolosa 9,
T915 213 896, www.restaurantecornucopia.
com, Metro Callao. Open daily. This
colourful, quirky restaurant is a real find:
changing art exhibits, crisp white tablecloths,
and fresh flowers on the tables. It's Spanish-
American owned, and serves modern
European food (and always a vegetarian
choice), and sublime desserts – don't miss
the strawberry mousse.

€€ Casa María, Plaza Mayor 23, T902 203
025. A reliable choice on the Plaza Mayor, this
serves fresh, market cuisine in an attractive,
brick-walled restaurant, which also has a
charming summer terrace out on the city's
most impressive square.

Tapas bars and cafés
Café de los Austrias, Plaza de Ramales 1,
T915 598 436, Metro Opera. Mon-Thu
0900-0130, Fri-Sat 0900-0230, Sun 0900-
2400. Large, old-fashioned café-bar with
marble columns and mirrors which is very
popular with locals. Perfect spot to while

away an afternoon or 3. Indifferent food, but perfect for coffee.

Café de Oriente, Plaza Oriente 2, T915 413 974, Metro Opera. Daily 0930-0130, until 0230 on Fri and Sat. Famous, chic café with a large terrace overlooking the square and the royal palace. There's an expensive restaurant, too, if you want to splash out for a special occasion.

Café La Union, C/Union 1, T915 425 563, Metro Opera. 1700-0300, until late on Fri and Sat, Sun 1700-0130. Stylish, airy café with changing art exhibitions, friendly staff and a mellow atmosphere – great place for a chat at any time. Fantastic *mojitos* – among the best in Madrid.

Mercado de San Miguel, Plaza de San Miguel s/n, T915 424 936, www.mercado desanmiguel.es. This pretty 19th-century glass-and-iron market is home to several excellent counter bars, serving a range of different tapas and speciality items, from wafer-thin Iberian ham to oysters or punnets of freshly fried fish.

Taberna del Cruzado, C/Amnistía 8, T915 480 131, Metro Opera. Closed Mon. This fancy gastro-bar has a beautiful carved wooden bar, dark red and cream walls, and charming staff. Among the unusual tapas are fried oyster mushrooms served with aioli, a kind of creamy garlic dip.

Plaza de Santa Ana and around *p38, maps p28 and p32*

Restaurants

€€€ Champagnería Gala, C/Moratín 22, T914 292 562, Metro Antón Martín. Valencian rice dishes including fantastic paella, served in a beautiful, glassy patio filled with plants and flowers. *Menú del día* is excellent value.

€€€-€€ El Txoko, C/Jovellanos 3, T915 323 443, Tue-Sat 1200-2300, Sun 1200-1500. Food served from 1400. Behind Cortes. Basque cuisine is celebrated throughout Spain, and the basement of the

Euskal Etxea (Basque Cultural Centre) is a great place for a delicious, budget lunch (*menú del día* €11), or some *pintxos* – pieces of French bread with toppings – at the bar.

€€ Le Petit Bistrot, Plaza de Matute, T914 296 255, www.lepetitbistrot.net. If you feel like a change from Spanish cuisine, head to this friendly bistro, and tuck into French onion soup, crêpes and quiches. Great set lunch deal available on weekdays.

€ La Biotika, C/Amor de Dios 3, T914 290 780, www.labiotika.es, Metro Antón Martín. Bright and airy café serving tasty vegetarian food, with plenty of dishes featuring seitan and tofu. *Menú del día* at just €10.90.

Tapas bars and cafés

The *tapeo* – a kind of bar crawl from tapas bar to tapas bar – is an institution in Madrid.

Bar Manolo, C/Jovellanos 7, T915 214 516. Daily except Sun and Mon evening 0830-2400. This old-fashioned local just behind the Cortes and in front of the Teatro de Zarzuela is a big favourite with local politicians and journalists, who huddle together in the little dining room at the back. The big thing here is *croquetas* – they are among the best in the city.

Casa Alberto, C/Huertas 18, T914 299 356, www.casaalberto.es. Open 1200-2400. Established in 1827, nothing much has changed at this steadfastly traditional tapas bar and restaurant. Friendly waiters in long white aprons scuttle efficiently between low wooden tables, and the walls are covered in kitsch paintings and old black and white photos of football teams and matadors. The house speciality is *cazuela rabo de toro* – ox tail stew, and the *albondigas* (meatballs) also come highly recommended.

La Dolores, Plaza de Jésus 4, T914 292 243. Open until 0100. Beautiful, century-old tiled tapas bar – one of the most *típico* in the city, and always jam-packed.

La Fábrica, C/Jesús 2, T913 690 671. Open 1100-0100. A cheerful, down to earth locals' bar with bright orange walls and a massive range of tapas. The counters groan with a dizzying array of canapés – slices of French bread loaded with all kinds of toppings from smoked salmon to cheese and quince jelly – and an octopus steams away on top of the counter.

Las Bravas, C/Espoz y Mina 13, T915 213 507, www.lasbravas.com. This is the home of *patatas bravas* – fried potatoes served with a (patented) sickly pinkish sauce. Neon-lit and garish, it's strictly for fast-food lovers – but the elderly waiters in their orange overalls are a cheerful bunch. Four branches, all within a few metres of each other.

Prado and Triangulo del Arte *p40, maps p28 and p32*
Tapas bars and cafés
Hotel Ritz, Plaza de la Lealtad 5, T917 016 767, Metro Banco de España. Treat yourself to tea at the *Ritz*; sink into a plush wicker chair in the enclosed gardens and forget the hoi polloi outside.

La Platería, C/Moratín 49, T914 291 722, Metro Atocha or Banco de España. Open til 0200. A relaxed, stylish tapas bar right across from the Prado, which overlooks a small square. It's enormously popular so get there early if you want a seat on the shady terrace.

La Latina and Lavapiés *p48, maps p28 and p32*
Restaurants
€€€ Casa Lucio, Cava Baja 35, T913 653 252, Metro La Latina, closed sat lunchtimes and Aug. Celebrated, typically Madrileño restaurant which is so popular, it's had to open another dining area across the street. The original space is the most atmospheric; this is the place to try Madrid-style tripe, or *cocido*.

€ Delic, Plaza de la Paja s/n, T913 645 450. A charming and stylish café, frequented by actors and writers, this serves delicious light meals, cakes and salads during the day, and cocktails by night.

€ El Estragón, Plaza de la Paja 10, T913 658 992, Metro La Latina. Friendly, pretty vegetarian restaurant set over several levels overlooking one of Madrid's loveliest squares. The food is very creative, using unusual combinations of ingredients.

€ La Musa Latina, Costanilla de San Andrés 12, T913 540 255, Metro La Latina, open Mon-Wed 0900-2400, Thu 0900-0100, Fri and Sat 1300-0200. This huge, stylish restaurant-café-tapas bar is right on Plaza de la Paja. New York loft meets the Far East in the decor, and the food is equally eclectic and extremely good.

Tapas bars and cafés
Ciné Doré, C/Santa Isabel 3, T913 694 923, Metro Antón Martín. 1700-2400, closed Mon. This pretty café attached to the art deco cinema has a terrace where films are shown on summer evenings. Good salads and snacks.

Matritum, C/Cava Alta 16, T915 283 662. A fantastic spot for wine-lovers, this has a huge selection of national wines, including several from unusual and hard-to-find labels. Delicious gourmet tapas, too.

Taberna Almendro, C/Almendro 13, T913654252, Metro La Latina. 1300-1600 and 1900-1200. Old-fashioned, friendly spot with ochre walls hung with wooden racks full of sherry glasses and oak barrels for tables; house specialities include *roscas* (a kind of round, well stuffed sandwich) and, more surprisingly, egg, bacon and chips (a great hangover cure). Excellent olives, too.

Taberna Tempranillo, Cava Baja 38, T913641532, closed Easter week and Aug, Metro La Latina. 1200-1600 and 2000-0100. A paddle fan flaps lazily, and there's a vast wall of wine bottles behind the bar. An excellent selection of wines, including weekly specials, and a good (if pricey) menu of cured meats and regional cheeses, including a contender for smelliest cheese ever – La Perbal from Asturias.

Gran Vía, Chueca and Malasaña *p51, maps p28 and p32*

Restaurants

€€€ Café Oliver, C/Almirante 12, T915 217 379. Metro Banco de España. A chic bistro, popular with actors and literary types, and famous across the city for its fabulous weekend brunches.

€€€ La Castafiore, C/Barquillo 30, T915322100, Metro Chueca. Elegant and traditional, but entirely unstuffy, this charming restaurant features Basque cuisine; the food is excellent but the real draw is the waiters, who perform opera and *zarzuela* at weekends.

€€ Bar Tomate, C/Fernando el Santo 26, T917 023 870. This fashionable bistro features pared-down wooden décor, and serves a choice of tapas or full meals. Delicious Mediterranean cuisine is on the menu, prepared with whatever's freshest in season.

€€ Bocaíto, C/Libertad 6, T915 321 219. Closed Aug. With its colourful tiles, and old-fashioned décor, this is a great place for traditional, Spanish fare, from hearty winter stews to freshly made tapas.

€ La Isla del Tesoro, C/Manuel Malasaña 3, T915931440, Metro Bilbao. Closed Sun and lunchtimes during holidays. Exotic bamboo screens, sea shells and deep blue walls make this a wonderfully romantic spot; it's vegetarian, and the well-priced *menú del día* (€11) features the cuisine of a different country each day.

Tapas bars and cafés

Bar Casa do Compañeiro, C/San Vicente Ferrer 44, T915 215 702. This is a tiled, slightly battered old tapas bar run by a friendly Galician family. There's plenty of *pulpo*

(octopus) and other fish on the menu, and they also serve crisp, cold *vermut* from the barrel.

Bodegas de Ángel Sierra, C/Gravina 11, T935 310 126, Metro Chueca. 1030-1600 and 1900-2300. Ancient, delightfully old-fashioned bar with battered dark wooden fittings and a marble counter; *vermut* on tap, perfectly accompanied with a *tapa* of anchovy and olive.

Bodegas El Maño, C/de la Palma 64, T915 215 057. Wonderfully old-fashioned, this long-established classic is ideal for a refreshing vermut (vermouth), poured straight from the barrel, and accompanied by some delicious, classic tapas.

Café Acuarela, C/Gravina 10, T915 222 143, Metro Chueca. Nymphs, cherubs, candle light and candelabra; great cocktails. Get there early to get a seat. Gay-run with a mixed gay/straight crowd.

Café Comercial, Glorieta de Bilbao 7, T915 215 655, Metro Bilbao. Daily 0730-0100 until 0200 Fri and Sat. Huge, famous, scruffy old café with outdoor tables in summer, mirrors and marble-topped tables; there's an internet area upstairs, too.

Café de Ruiz, C/Ruiz 11, T914 461 232, Metro Bilbao. 1230-0230. A local institution, set in a series of small salons, with plush sofas, low lighting and dark wooden fittings. Good for cakes, coffee and cocktails.

Café Figueroa, C/Augusto Figueroa 17, T915 229 688. Until 0230 at weekends. An elegant 19th-century café which has become a classic on the gay scene – a great first-stop in Madrid.

Café Manuela, C/San Vicente Ferrer 29, T915 317 037, Metro Tribunal. Mon-Thu 1800-0200, Fri-Sun 1600-0230. Large, lush Art Nouveau-style café, live music, story-telling nights, poetry readings and *tertulias*.

El Jardín Secreto, C/Conde Duque 2, T915 418 023, Metro Plaza de España. Mon-Thu 1730-0100, Fri-Sat 1800-0230, Sun 1700-2400. Magical, tranquil café with rattan furniture and a scattering of shells, candles, and hazy drapes.

El Pez Gordo, C/Pex 6, T915 223 208, Metro Noviciado. Mon-Sat 2000-0130, until 0230 Fri and Sat. Fat Fish (which in Spanish means something like our the Big Cheese) is a fairly ordinary tapas bar made extraordinary by its delicious food and its entertaining and very theatrical clientele.

La Musa, C/Manuela Malasaña 18, T914 487 558, Metro Bilbao. Hugely popular with a young, lively crowd, this cellar tapas bar serves up excellent and very imaginative tapas and *raciones*.

Salamanca *p55, map p28*
Restaurants

€€€ Zalacaín, C/Alvarez de Baena 4, T915 614 840, Metro Gregorio Marañón. Closed Sat lunchtimes, Sun, holidays, Holy Week, Aug. Madrid's most celebrated classic restaurant, holder of all kinds of stars and awards. Chef Benjamín Urdiaín can't put a foot wrong, it seems; cuisine, service and decor ooze elegance and assurance.

€€ Paradis Casa-América, Paseo de Recoletos 2, T915 754 540, Metro Banco de España. Closed Sat lunchtimes, Sun and holidays. Located in the Palacio de Linares, this attractive tiled restaurant with a leafy summer terrace is a favourite with businessmen at lunchtimes, when it serves a good-value *menú del día*. Rice dishes are the house speciality.

€€ Teatriz, C/Hermosilla 15, T915 775 379, Metro Serrano. Philip Starck and Javier Mariscal famously converted this theatre during the last years of La Movida. After another spectacular revamp, it's still the place to see and be seen.

€€ Thai Gardens, C/Jorge Juan 5, T915 778 884. Open until 0100 at weekends. Beautiful, deeply romantic restaurant decorated with traditional Thai crafts and silks; decent Thai although not especially authentic.

Tapas bars and cafés

Café del Espejo, Paseo de Recoletos 33, T913082347, Metro Colón. 1030-0100, closed Sat lunch. It may look the part, but this café is in fact a recent arrival. The art nouveau-style swirls may be fake, but it's still a beautiful.

Café Gijón, Paseo de Recoletos 21, T915 215 425, Metro Banco de España. One of the oldest and loveliest cafés in Madrid, still haunted by the ghosts of 19th-century *tertulias*. Tapas, *raciones* and meals are also available.

Embassy, Paseo de la Castellana 12, T914 359 480, Metro Colón. 0930-0100. This chi chi delicatessen also has a delightful café where you can tuck into cakes with the ladies who lunch.

Le Cabrera, Paseo de Recoletos 2, T913 199 457. Perhaps the most fashionable spot in town, this serves spectacularly imaginative (if pricey) tapas and raciones created by super-chefs Sergi Arola and Ben Bensoussan, as well as fabulous cocktails. Located in the sumptuous **Casa de América** (page 55), they also run the excellent and equally glamorous restaurant, **Cien Llaves** (**€€€**).

Los Timbales, C/Alcalá 227, T917 250 768, Metro Ventas. Crammed with bull-fighting memorabilia, this is the classic stop-off before or after a *corrida*. Good tapas, including the house speciality, *timbales* or pies stuffed with meat or cheese, and a terrace in summer.

🎧 Bars and clubs

Madrid's legendary nightlife may have gone off the boil since the giddy days of La Movida, but it's still among the best in Europe. The club scene is raging, with international DJs as well as plenty of homegrown ones, and there's something for everyone. The city council have been doing their best for the last few years to stamp out the so-called 'after hours' clubs which carried on when the regular clubs were closing their doors at dawn, but it's still perfectly possible to start dancing on Fri night and not stop until Mon morning. Most of the

One-stop-shop...

Some of the hippest new places on the Madrid scene are the slickly designed restaurant-bar-club combos. These are some of the best:

Alquimia, C/ Villanueva 2, T915 772 785, Metro Retiro. Lounge about in deep leather sofas, or dine in faux-Gothic splendour. Wear your Manolos.

Larios Café, C/Silva 4, T915 479 394, Metro Santo Domingo or Callao. Gorgeous, award-winning art deco-esque interior; Cuban food in the restaurant and salsa, flamenco and funk on the dancefloor.

Lolita Lounge And Bar, C/Manuel Falla 3, T913 441 156, www.lolitalounge.net, Metro Santiago Bernabeu. Sushi bar, cocktails and two floors of dance music – everything from 1970s classics to UK and Spanish house and garage. Worth dressing up for.

Suite Café-Club, C/Virgen de los Peligros 4, T915 214 031, Metro Sevilla. Plenty of film stars at this favourite with the so-cool-it-hurts crowd; sharp 1970s-style decor, good global fusion cuisine in the restaurant, cool ambient sounds on one dance floor and deep house on the other.

---

really big clubs can be found along the Gran Vía and the Paseo Castellano, but Madrid also has hundreds of *discobares*, bars with DJs and small dance floors, spread all over the city.

To get the latest, visit www.clubbingin spain.com, which has listings for upcoming events and club nights.

Old Madrid *p30, maps p28 and p32*

Belmondo, C/Caños Viejos 3, T913 663 013, http://belmondococktails.com. The contemporary design and superb cocktails are crowd-pleasers, but it's the wonderful terrace that makes this one of the most popular bars in town.

Joy Eslava, C/Arenal 11, T913 663 733, Metro Opera. This converted theatre became one of the biggest clubs of the Movida years. The fashion pack have moved on but it's still fun for an over-the-top night out.

Kathmandu, C/Señores de Luzón 3, T600 483 293, Metro Sol and Opera. Great funk, friendly crowd, and cool DJs at this groovy, red-painted subterranean bar and club.

Plaza de Santa Ana and around *p38, map p30 and p34*

Cardamomo, C/Echegaray 15, T913 690 757, Metro Sevilla, daily 2100-0400. Despite its

dated look – all vintage posters and dodgy memorabilia – this is a cool spot which offers regular live music, including some excellent jazz, flamenco and salsa.

Glass Bar/La Terraza (in the **Hotel Urban**), Carrera de San Jerónimo 34, T91 787 7770. If you want to get dressed up and hang out with the city's fashion pack, this swanky hotel is the place to do it. The rooftop bar, La Terraza, comes into its own in summer, with DJs.

The Penthouse (in the **Hotel Me by Meliá**), Plaza de Santa Ana 14, T917 016 000. Another of the city's hot hotel bars, this has some of the best views in town. Fabulous cocktails, top notch DJs, and an ultra chic crowd.

Viva Madrid, C/Fernandez Gonzalez 7, T914 203 596, Metro Sol or Sevilla. Huge, beautifully tiled bar on 2 levels, with paddle fans, some simple tapas, and DJ sessions at weekends. An ex-pat favourite, with a summer terrace and pricey drinks.

Prado and Triangulo del Arte *p40, map p30 and p34*

Teatro Kapital, C/Atocha 125, T914 202 906, Metro Atocha, Fri-Sun and public holidays 1730-2300, 2400-0600. Huge, fun, mega-club on several floors.

La Latina and Lavapiés *p48, map p30 and p34*

Aloque, C/Torrecilla del Leal 20, T915 283 662. It is amazing that such a minuscule bar can pack in such a huge selection of wines – more than 1000 labels are on offer, along with tapas and raciones.

Delic, Costanilla de San Andrés, Plaza de Paja 14, T913 645 450. Metro La Latina. Closed Sun, Mon. This retro-looking spot is a relaxing café by day and a busy, very stylish bar by night.

El Bonnano, Plaza Humilladero 4, Metro La Latina, T913 666 886. There's always a trendy young crowd propping up this little bar overlooking the wide square. Bright modern art hangs on the walls, some basic snacks and a mellow soundtrack.

El Mojito, C/Olmo 6, Metro Lavapiés. Excellent music, lively gay/mixed crowd, a popular spot with the fashion pack.

Gaudeamus, Edificio Escuelas Pías, C/Tribulete 14, 4th floor, T915 282 594. A fantastic rooftop bar and restaurant where you can soak up the views of the city skyline over a few beers.

Ventura Club, C/Olmo 31, T914 680 454, Metro Antón Martín. You'd never think it from the outside, but this is one of the best places for drum 'n' bass, electronica and trip hop.

Gran Vía, Chueca and Malasaña *p51, map p30 and p34*

Camp, C/Marqués de Valdeiglesias 6, T915 319 215, Metro Chueca. Closed Sun-Thu. Glassy café-bar full of self- consciously beautiful people reclining on 70s style furniture. Attracts a mixed crowd.

Chicote, Gran Vía 12, T915 326 737, Metro Gran Vía. Closed Sun. The grandaddy of all Madrileño cocktail bars, famously a favourite with Ava Gardner and Frank Sinatra. Chicote has preserved its stunning art deco decor and its impossibly glamorous air.

Cock, C/Reina 16, T915 322 826. Begun by a bar tender trained at Chicote, Cock is equally glamorous and chi chi. Order the speciality of the house – an exquisite gin fizz.

El Café de la Palma, C/Palma 62, T915 225 031, www.cafedelapalma.com, Metro Noviciado. Excellent chill-out area at the back, comfortable booths in the main area and regular live gigs. Café and bar.

Goa/Ohm/Bash, Plaza Callao 4, Metro Callao. Same place, different club nights. One of the best venues in Madrid, with pumping music, go go dancers, and a gay/mixed, slickly dressed clientele.

La Ida, C/Colón 11, T915 229 107, Metro Tribunal. Relaxed, arty little café-bar which serves fantastic tea and cakes by day, and gets packed out in the evenings and at weekends.

Mondo at Stella, C/Arlabán 7, T915 327 833, Metro Noviciado and Plaza de España. Thu, Sat only. This massively popular club night is held in Stella, one of the big stars of the Movida. One of the best nights out in the city.

Santamaría, La Coctelería de Al Lado, C/Ballesta 6. A popular, boho-chic bar in the trendy Chueca district, great for cocktails. Get here early: it gets a bit hectic later on.

Salamanca *p55, map p30 and p34*

Serrano 41, C/Serrano 41, T915 781 865, www.serrano41.es. A popular club in the Salamanca district, which boasts a great outdoor terrace in summer.

Teatríz, C/Hermosilla 15, T915 775 379, Metro Serrano. Philip Starck's and Mariscal's designer bar set in a converted theatre. One of the best-known in the city.

⊕ Entertainment

The weekly guide *La Guia del Ocio* (Spanish only) is available from kiosks and has extensive theatre, music and opera listings. It's pretty good for live music too, but downright rubbish when it comes to clubs and bars. For what's going on in Madrid's ever-changing nightlife, get flyers from the Mercado del Fuencarral (see below) or pick up a copy of the English-language monthly newspaper *InMadrid*, www.inmadrid.com, which reviews bars and clubs in English. The free *What's On* guide from the tourist office has some cultural listings in English. On Fridays, *El Mundo* and *ABC* both produce entertainment supplements which can be useful, and you can pick up the freebie *LaNetro* in most shops (all in Spanish).

Cinema

The cinema is cheap by most European standards, and is cheaper still on the *día del espectador* ('spectator's day'), usually Mon or Wed.

Cine Capitol, Gran Vía 41, T902 333 231, Metro Callao. One of several beautiful old cinemas from the beginning of the 20th century. Films are usually dubbed.

Cine Doré (Filmoetca Nacional), C/Santa Isabel 3, T915 490 011, Metro Antón Martín. Ticket office open 1600-2245, bookshop open 1700-2230, bar-restaurant 1600-2400. The home of the National Film Institute, this endearing Art Deco cinema puts on a varied programme of classics, foreign-language films and film festivals. Outdoor screenings on the roof terrace in summer.

Pequeño Cine Estudio, C/Magallanes 1, T914 472 920, www.pcinestudio.es, Metro Quevedo. Arthouse cinema showing a range of international films plus some cult classics.

Classical and contemporary dance

As a major European capital, Madrid hosts the finest dance companies from around the world and you might also get a chance to see the Madrid-based Ballet Nacional de Espanya (Spanish National Ballet), or the more contemporary Compañía Nacional de Danza. The annual **Madrid en Danza festival** (see page 69) is a good time to check out up-and-coming dance groups.

Sala Cuarto Pared, C/Ercilla 7, Arganzuela, T915 172 317, www.cuartapared.es, Metro Embajadores. This is one of the best venues in Madrid for contemporary dance, and is also a good place to find experimental drama productions.

Teatro Fernán Gómez, Plaza de Colón s/n, T914 362 540, Metro Colón. Madrid's main municipal arts centre, with an interesting programme of dance, music, and drama. It regularly hosts *zarzuela* during the summer, and is one of the main venues for Madrid en Danza.

Teatro Real, Plaza de Isabel II, T915 160 660, Metro Opera. Madrid's beautifully restored opera house (see page 36) provides an opulent venue for opera and ballet.

Flamenco

Madrid's flamenco scene is as vibrant as anywhere in Spain; there are dozens of places to hear and see flamenco in all its styles, from the most traditional to the latest trends.

Candela, C/Olmo 2, T914 673 382, Metro Antón Martín. A celebrated flamenco bar which hosts occasional performances and is very popular with flamenco artists and those who come to gawp at them. The atmosphere gets better as it gets later.

Casa Patas, C/Cañizares 10, T913 690 496, Metro Antón Martín. The stage is in a shadowy, intimate little room at the back of the bar-restaurant area; it's small enough to feel the sweat of the performers as they whirl about the stage, and no one can help joining in with the odd 'olé'. The flamenco performances are among the best in the city.

La Soleá, Cava Baja 27, T913 653 308, Metro La Latina. Anything can happen at this famous flamenco bar where guitarists and singers gather for semi-impromptu performances. You won't be alone – the bar is propped up mostly by 'guiris' (young foreigners) nowadays – yet it still retains a magical atmosphere.

Las Carboneras, Plaza del Conde de Miranda 1, T915 428 677, Metro Sol. Flamenco tablao, which has breathtakingly skilful dancers, musicians and singers, but is slightly lacking in atmosphere.

Peña Chaquetón, C/Canarias 39, T916 712 777, Metro Palos de la Frontera. Performances on Fri nights only, but get there early or you won't have a hope of getting in. It may be basic, but this is generally considered to be one of the very best flamenco venues in the city.

Football
Estadio del Rayo Vallecano, Arroyo del Olivar 49, T914 782 253, www.rayovalle cano.es, Metro Portazgo. Rayo Vallecano's home stadium.
Estadio Santiago Bernabeu, Paseo de la Castellana 104, T913 984 300, www.real madrid.es, Metro Santiago Bernabeu. Real Madrid's stadium.
Estadio Vicente Calderón, T902 260 403, www.clubatleticodemadrid.com, Metro Pirámides. Atlético de Madrid play here.

Music: classical and opera
Auditorio Nacional de Música, C/Príncipe de Vergara, T913 370 140 , www.auditorio nacional.mcu.es. Metro Cruz de Rayo or Prosperidad. Home of Spain's national choir and orchestra, and Madrid's main venue for classical music. Tickets available at the box office, online at www.entradasinaem.es or by phone at T902 224 949.
Fundación Juan March, C/Castelló 77, T914 354 240, Metro Núñez de Balboa. This exhibition space hosts regular chamber concerts and recitals, including lunchtime concerts which are usually free.
Teatro Real, Plaza de Isabel II, T915 160 660, Metro Opera. Madrid's beautifully restored opera house provides an opulent venue for opera and ballet, see also page 36.

Music: contemporary
Café Central, Plaza del Angel 10, T913 694 143. One of Madrid's loveliest jazz venues, set in an elegant, art deco café. Local and international groups play in the evening, but even if you don't catch a live show, it's the perfect place to while away an afternoon.
La Coquette, C/Hileras 14, T915 308 095, Metro Opéra. Tiny underground blues bar which fulfils every cliché in the book – smoky, louche and loud.
La Riviera, Paseo Bajo Virgen del Puerto s/n, Puente de Segovía, T913 652 415, Metro Puerta del Angel. Beautiful art deco-style concert venue near the river with a retractable roof. Mainly rock, indie and pop acts on the programme, but it has hosted some big international names. It doubles as a club, too.
Populart, C/Huertas 22, T914 298 407, Metro Antón Martin. Hugely popular, lively club featuring live jazz and blues, with occasional appearances by Latin and world music bands. It's got a great reputation and pulls in some well-known bands, but it's best during the week – weekends can get too crammed.
Sala Clamores, C/Albuquerque 14, T914 457 938, Metro Bilbao. Very popular jazz and world music venue.
Siroco, C/San Dimas 3, T91 593 3070, Metro Noviciado. All kinds of home-grown rock, indie and alternative bands show up on the programme of this laid-back music venue – which doubles up as an excellent little club.

Theatre
Madrid's theatrical tradition stretches back to the Golden Age of Lope de Vega, Calderón and Tirso de Molina, and the city is strewn with dozens of venues featuring all kinds of work from the traditional renditions of the classics to avant garde contemporary performances. For the most interesting contemporary performances, check out what's on at the **Sala Cuarto Pared** (listed above under Dance), **the Mirador** or the **Circulo de Bellas Artes**.
Circulo de Bellas Artes, C/Marqués de Casa Riera 2, T913 605 400, Metro Banco de España. This art deco exhibition space and café regularly hosts innovative performances.

Zarzuela

Zarzuela is Madrid's very own light operetta. It got its name from the Palace de la Zarzuela (on the outskirts of Madrid) where the earliest performances were created for the Philip IV and his court. The stories were usually sugary and sentimental, sometimes spiced up with a little contemporary gossip based on local events – one even describes the grand opening of the Gran Vía. They were hugely popular right up until the Civil War, but only just made it through the repressive years of Franco's dictatorship. Still, zarzuela has been enjoying a bit of a revival over the past couple of decades.

In summer, catch an outdoor performance at **Jardines de Sabatini** (see page 37). The delightful **Teatro de la Zarzuela** (C/Jovellanes 4, T915 245 400, http://teatro delazarzuela.mcu.es, Metro Banco de España) holds performances year round.

Teatro de la Comedia, C/Principe 14, T915 214 931, Metro Sol. Another grand theatre, this also hosts classical performances and is home to the Compañia Nacional de Teatro Clásico.

Teatro Español, C/Príncipe 25, T914 296 297, Metro Sol. Classical Spanish drama.

Teatro María Guerrero, C/Tamayo y Baus 4, T913 194 769, Metro Colon or Chueca. Just west of the Paseo de Recoletos, this beautiful old theatre is home to the Centro Dramático Nacional.

❂ Festivals and events

5 Jan Cabalgata de Los Reyes (Three Kings): in all Spanish towns, the Three Kings parade in floats tossing out sweets to children.

Feb Carnavales: plenty of dressing-up, floats, parades and street parties. The festivities finish up with the Burial of the Sardine (Entierro de la Sardina) to mark the end of winter.

Feb La Alternativa: an alternative theatre and dance festival held at venues throughout the city. It's held some time in Feb or Mar – check at the tourist office for exact dates.

Feb ARCO: massive, month-long, contemporary art fair.

Easter Semana Santa: Holy Week is celebrated with solemn processions and masses. Venerated statues are paraded through the streets by the different confra-ternities in their strange pointed hoods.

2 May Fiesta del dos de Mayo: celebrates its uprising against the Napoleonic forces with bands in the Plaza del Dos de Mayo, and events in the cultural venues.

8-15 May Fiestas de San Isidro: festivities for Madrid's patron saint, San Isidro, with parades. It also marks the opening of the bullfighting season, with several events.

May-Jun Madrid en Danza: international Dance Festival held in venues across the city.

Jun Fiesta de San Antonio de la Florida: Street party near the hermitage of San Antonio de la Florida, which is decorated with Goya's frescoes.

Jun Festimad, www.festimad.es: outdoor music festival held in the suburb of Mostoles.

Mid-Jun to mid-Jul PhotoEspaña: international photography festival, exhibitions, workshops and talks.

24 Jun Día de San Juan: this midsummer festival is not such big news in Madrid as it is elsewhere in Spain, but there are fireworks and musicians in the Parque del Buen Retiro.

Jul-Sep Veranos de la Villa (Summers in the City): the largest city-sponsored arts festival in Madrid, with a range of activities spanning theatre, dance and music.

6-15 Aug Verbenas de San Cayetano, San Lorenzo and La Paloma: these colourful, traditional street festivals take place in the old neighbourhoods of La Latina and Lavapiés.

Late Sep to Nov Festival de Otoño:
the Autumn Festival focuses on the
performing arts.
Nov (throughout) **Festival de Jazz de
Madrid**: Madrid's International Jazz festival
draws some big names and is very enjoyable.
9 Nov Fiesta de la Virgen de la Almudena:
Mass is held in the Plaza Mayor for the city's
female patron saint.
Dec Feria de Artesanía (Craft Fair): the
shops fill with traditional decorations for crib
scenes and there's a huge craft market held in
the Plaza de España.
31 Dec Noche Vieja (New Year): everyone
piles into the Puerta del Sol where it's
traditional to eat a grape for luck at each
chime of the clock at midnight.

◎ Shopping

As Spain's capital, Madrid contains every
kind of shop imaginable from excellent fresh
food markets to tiny old-fashioned shops
which haven't changed in decades, and
glitzy shopping malls where you can get
everything. It's also kitsch-lovers heaven
with a dazzling array of fabulous tack. You
can find almost anything you want in the
streets around C/Preciados in the centre –
department stores, chain stores, individual
shops selling everything from hams to
traditional Madrileño cloaks.

The northwest neighbourhoods of
Argüelles and Moncloa, particularly
C/Princesa, are also good for department
stores and fashion chains. The kiosks on
Puerta del Sol have newspapers. Smart
Salamanca has plenty of designer fashion
boutiques and interior decoration shops at
prices to make you gasp. Chueca is full of
hip, unusual fashion and music shops as
well as shoe-shoppers' heaven, the
C/Augusto Figueroa.

Books and newspapers
Fnac, C/Preciados 28, Metro Sol or Callao.
Massive store packed with books, DVDs, CDs
and electronic goods. There's also a travel
agency, a newspaper shop (with international
press), and a concert ticket agency.
Pasajes International Bookshop, C/Génova
3, Metro Alonso Martínez. Friendly bookshop
with a useful notice board (jobs or long-term
accommodation) and a good range of titles
in English.

Department stores and
shopping centres
ABC Serrano Centro Comercial, C/Serrano 61,
Metro Serrano. Shopping centre housed in the
former ABC newspaper building. The usual
array of fast food outlets and chain stores plus
a smattering of upmarket shops selling
household goods and fashion.
El Corte Inglés, C/Preciados 2-3, Metro Sol.
One of several branches of Spain's biggest
department store: fashion, toys, electrical
goods, and souvenirs plus a basement
supermarket and gourmet shop. Other
services include a caféteria, bureau de
change, travel agency, and ticket outlet.

Fashion and accessories
Camper, C/Preciados 75, Metro Argüelles.
There are branches of this popular shoe store
all over the city. Bright, comfortable, and
playful, somewhat cheaper than outside Spain.
Loewe, C/Serrano 34, Metro Serrano. Luxury
leather goods, and ultra-fashionable clothes
for men and women who don't have to look
at price tags. One of several luxury labels represented on this street and those around it.
Mango, C/Arenal 24, Metro Opera. Another
runaway Spanish chain, Mango offers the latest
women's fashions in decent fabrics.
Zara, C/Gran Vía 32, Metro Callao. You are
never far from a branch of this fashion chain
which is the best bet for stylish clothes, shoes
and accessories at really low prices.

Food and drink
Casa Mira, C/San Jerónimo 30, Metro Sol.
Lovely, old-fashioned baker which sells all

kinds of goodies, displayed on a revolving glass stand. It's the place to buy *turrón*, a delicious honey-flavoured soft nougat, which is traditionally eaten around Christmas.

Convento de las Carboneras, C/Codo, Metro La Latina or Sol. This is a little hard to find, tucked down a small passageway just off the Plaza del Villa. Press the buzzer marked *monjas* (nuns) and you will ushered down a corridor and given a list of *dulces* (sweet things) to choose from. The money is put into a revolving drum, and your cakes and change will come out the other side.

Mantequerías Gonzalez, C/León 12, Metro Antón Martín. Fabulous range of gourmet deli items (and a very pleasant little bar area at the back to try some of them out). Wines, olive oils, luxurious tins and jars of anchovies and other delicacies (good presents) and a great range of cheeses and cured meats. Very friendly staff.

Markets

Cuesta de Claudio Moyano, Metro Atocha. Second-hand book stalls line this pretty street near Atocha station. Most open daily and are always good for a rummage.

El Rastro (see page 50). Madrid's legendary Sunday morning flea market.

Mercado de San Miguel, Plaza de San Miguel, Metro Sol. Set in a turn-of-the-century listed building, this is probably Madrid's prettiest market. Dozens of stalls sell all kinds of superb gourmet produce from fish to cheese with a fantastic array of cured meats.

Mercado de Sellos y Monedas (stamp and coin market), Metro Sol. Plaza Mayor on Sun mornings.

Souvenirs and unusual shops

Casa Seseña, C/Cruz 23, Metro Sol. This delightful old shop is the only place left in Madrid which still makes the traditional Madrileño cloaks.

El Flamenco Vive, C/Conde de Lemos 7, Metro Opera. Specialist flamenco shop with a fantastic range of books and CDs as well as guitars and percussion instruments. This is also the place to come to find out what's really going on in the flamenco scene, with lots of flyers and posters.

La Tienda de Real Madrid, Centro Comercial La Esquina del Bernabéu, C/Concha Espina 1. A mecca for football fans – strips, scarves, caps and a whole host of other memorabilia emblazened with Real Madrid's logo.

Maty, C/Maestro Victoria 2, Metro Opera. Packed with flouncy flamenco dresses, shoes, hair-combs, clackable castanets and various other accessories. The tiny dresses for little girls are adorable.

⚠ What to do

Check both the municipal and regional tourist offices for details of the tours they offer.

Bus tours

Juliatur, Gran Vía 68, T902 024 443, www.juliatravel.com. Tours around Madrid, including night-time tours, plus excursions to the towns around the city. Prices vary according to the tour.

Madrid Tour, T902 024 578, www.madrid citytour.es. A hop-on hop-off bus service with multilingual commentary. Adult €21 for one day.

Pullmantur, Plaza de Oriente 8, T915 411 805. Also offer a wide selection of tours, both within the city centre and further afield. Prices vary.

Cycling tours

Bravo Bike.com, C/Juan Alvare Mendizábel 19, T915 582 945, www.bravobike.com. A very friendly outfit which will collect you from your hotel and provide all equipment. A range of bicycle tours (with multilingual guides), in Madrid and around (El Escorial, Segovia and La Granja, Chinchón and Aranjuez, mountain-biking in the Sierras).

Jogging

Jardin Retiro (see page 46) is the shadiest and most attractive area to jog in the city centre. **Casa de Campo** (see page 54) has acres of unspoilt woodland. Also well known for prostitution, but this tends to take place close to the roads.

Language schools

Acento Español, C/Mayor 4, 6º9, T915 213 676, www.acentoespanol.com. Intensive and general courses, preparation for official DELE exam. Can arrange accommodation.
CEE Idiomas, C/Carmen 6, T915 211 004, www.cee-idiomas.com. Courses for all levels, preparation for DELE, cultural activities.

Sports centres

The following municipal sports centres all have outdoor pools, gyms, tennis courts and other sports.
Casa de Campo, Av del Angel, s/n, T914630050, Metro Lago or Puerta del Ángel.
La Elipa, Prolongación de O'Donnell s/n, T914 303 511, Metro La Estrella.
Vicente del Bosque, Av de Monforte de Lemos, s/n, T913 147 943, Metro Barrio del Pilar or Begoña

Walking

Municipal Tourist Office, see page 27, offers a vast array of walking tours, outlined in a free booklet.

Yoga

Centro de Yoga Avagar, C/Bravo Murillo 243, 1st floor, T915 797 282, www.avagar.com. Kundalini yoga; also offers a range of natural therapies.

⊖ Transport

Air

See Getting to Madrid and Central Spain, page 6, for airport information.

Bus and metro

Bus and metro plans are available at tourist offices, at metro and bus stations, or online at www.ctm-madrid.es (which also provides information on suburban bus and rail services if you are planning a day trip to Toledo or Segovia, for example). A single ticket for one trip by bus or metro costs €0.95, or you can get a *Metrobús ticket* (which can be shared) for €12.20 which is valid for 10 journeys on the bus or metro. Buy single tickets at metro and bus stations, and the *Metrobús* ticket is also sold at tobacconists (*estancos*).

Car

Be aware, cars with foreign number plates or Spanish rental cars are prime targets for thieves. Renting a car is a good idea if you want to explore the area around Madrid, particularly the Sierra de Guadarrama. The best deals are usually online, and you should find out if the airline you fly with offers car rental deals.

Offices of the major car rental companies can be found at the airport, and the 2 main train stations, Atocha and Chamartín.

Details as follows: **Avis**, T902 180 854, www.avis.com; **Europcar**, T902 105 030, www.europcar.com; Hertz, T902 402 405, www.hertz.es; **National/Atesa**, T902 100 101, www.national.com, www.atesa.es.

Cycling

Cycling in the city centre is only for the brave, although it can be fun to cycle around parks like the Buen Retiro or the huge Casa del Campo. For bike tours, see page 71. There's some excellent mountain-biking in the Sierras around the city, see page 76.

Taxi

There are plenty in Madrid. White with a red stripe on the front doors, they can be hailed at the Puerta del Sol or near the metro station at Opera. Prices are reasonable, but there are supplements for luggage, pets, and after 2200 and at weekends.

Train

Regional trains (*cercanías*) usually call at both Atocha and Chamartín stations, but note that the high-speed *AVE* trains for **Sevilla** and **Córdoba** leave from Atocha. See under individual town entries for details of train services.

❶ Directory

Banks and ATMs

Banks and ATMS (look for a sign saying *telebanco*) are everywhere. You'll find several banks on the Puerta del Sol, the Gran Vía and around the Plaza España.

Hospitals

Hospital Clínico Universitario San Carlos, C/Profesor Martin Lagos s/n, T913 303 000, Metro Moncloa.
Hospital General Gregorio Marañon, C/Dr. Esquerdo, 46, T915 868 000, Metro O'Donnell.
Hospital La Princesa Del Insalud, C/Diego De Leon, 62, T915 202 200, Metro Diego de León.
Madrid Health Centre, C/Lagasca 104, T617 041 936, www.madridhealth center.com. English speaking.

Pharmacies

Pharmacies have a list of the 24-hr pharmacies in their windows. The following are open 24 hrs: **Real Botica de la Reina Madre**, C/Mayor 59, T915 480 014, Metro Opera; **Farmacia de la Paloma**, C/ Toledo 46, T913 653 458, Metro La Latina; **Farmacia del Globo**, C/Atocha 46, Metro Antón Martín; **Farmacia Goya**, C/ Goya 89, T914 354 958, Metro Goya.

Post

The main post office is at Paseo del Pardo 1, T915 230 694, information T902 197 197, www.correos.es. Mon-Fri 0830-2130, Sat 0830-1400. Postboxes, marked *Correos y Telégrafos*, are yellow. Most tobacconists (*estancos*, marked with a brown and yellow symbol) sell stamps.

Central Spain

Madrileños abandon the capital at weekends for their second homes in the pretty mountain villages of Navacerrada and Cotos, where there is plenty of hiking, climbing and even skiing. Backed by a startling mountainous backdrop, Segovia is one of the loveliest cities in Spain, famous for its sturdy Castillian cuisine and the vast Roman aqueduct. Ávila, known as the 'City of Saints and Stones', is quieter and more contemplative, hemmed in by a remarkable ring of medieval fortified walls. Behind it stretches the wild and remote Sierra de Gredos, a spectacular mountain range with tiny stone villages and excellent hiking trails.

When the kings and queens of Spain wanted respite from the capital's burning heat, they took themselves off to palaces and hunting lodges: the Habsburgs preferred the sombre austerity of El Escorial, but the Bourbons built fanciful Baroque extravaganzas at La Granja de San Ildefonso and Aranjuez, and surrounded them with exquisite gardens. The extensive gardens of Aranjuez are especially beautiful, a rare and refreshing oasis of green in the burning Castillian plain.

The ancient university town of Alcalá de Henares was the birthplace of Cervantes, whose home has been converted into an engaging little museum, but the old streets are still smattered with magnificent Renaissance architecture. The hilltop city of Toledo remains the most popular day-trip from Madrid and with good reason: Romans, Visigoths, Muslims, Jews and Christians have all left their mark on this famously tolerant and cultured city and the tiny streets and passages which twist around the enormous cathedral are still redolent of the city's glorious past.

Getting around

Some of the towns and villages described below fall into the province of the Comunidad de Madrid, which forms a donut-shaped ring around the capital city, but many of them don't: Ávila, Segovia and the villages of Sierra de Gredos are in Castilla y León, perfect stopping points on the way to the castles and wine regions of Northern Spain; Toledo is in Castilla-La Mancha, close to Don Quijote territory for anyone who wants to follow the footsteps of Spain's most famous literary figure.

El Escorial and the Sierra de Guadarrama → *For listings, see pages 98-105.*

The spiky peaks of the Sierra de Guadarrama are visible even from Madrid. This is where Felipe II chose to build his vast, forbidding palace-monastery, in a crook in the hills 42 km northwest of Madrid. A couple of kilometres away is Franco's own burial place and monument to the fallen of the Civil War (close enough to the Royal Pantheon to satisfy any ego). The villages of the Sierra are stuffed full of Madrileño second homes, and are good bases for walking, mountain-biking and even skiing.

Real Monasterio de San Lorenzo el Real de El Escorial

ⓘ *www.patrimonionacional.es, open Tue-Sun 1000-2000, winter (Oct-Mar) until 1800; Gardens, the Casita del Príncipe, and the Castia del Infante (see below) are open until one hour earlier. €10/€5, guided visit €7, audioguide €4. Café and shop. The information office opposite the monastery entrance has details on trekking, horse riding and balloon rides in the area.*

The lugubrious monastery is enormous and chilly, even in the height of summer. Few admit to liking it – the 19th-century French writer Théophile Gaultier went so far as to say that its visitors could amuse themselves for the rest of their lives with the thought that they could be in El Escorial but were not – but none can fail to be impressed by the staggering proportions: 16 patios, 15 cloisters, nine towers, 1200 doors and 2600 windows.

The tour begins at the **Bourbon apartments** in the northeast section of the palace. Gloomy El Escorial was far too depressing for the frivolous Bourbons who spent little time here, but their apartments contain some beautiful tapestries by Goya. Two museums are housed in the cellars beneath these rooms: the Museo de Pintura, with works by Veronese, Titian, van Dyck, Rubens, van der Weyden and Ribera, among others; and the Museum of Architecture, which shows the original plans for the monastery along with some of the equipment used for hauling the huge hunks of granite.

The **Habsburg apartments** are unexpectedly intimate, prettily decorated with blue and white tiles. You can see the specially designed chair in which gout-ridden Felipe II was carried by his long-suffering servants, who had to put up with the stench of their master's gouty leg as well as his manic eccentricities, and the bed in which he died in 1598, carefully placed so that he could hear Mass from the basilica directly below.

When Felipe died, he was buried in the **Panteón de los Reyes** (Royal Pantheon), where a dozen Spanish monarchs are buried in a flurry of gold and marble. Next to the pantheon is the **Rotting Room** (sealed off, thankfully), where the bodies of dead monarchs were left to rot and dry out before being placed in the Pantheon.

The **Salas Capitulares** (Chapter Halls) contain more of El Escorial's enormous art collection, gathered underneath elaborately painted 16th-century ceilings. The Basilica is the very heart of the complex, repressively dark, cold and gloomy. It contains 43 altars so that several masses could be held at the same time; just two chapels, right at the back, were for commoners.

Around the monastery

After staggering out of the monastery, most visitors want to make for the nearest bar. **Calle Floridablanca** is one of the most animated streets, with several tapas bars and restaurants, and the added delight of the **Real Coliseo**, a charming little theatre built for Carlos III. There are two small palaces downhill towards El Escorial proper, both plush Bourbon fripperies: the **Casita del Príncipe** (or the Casita Abajo) ① *guided tours Apr-Sep Tue-Sun 1000-1800, Oct-Mar Tue-Sun 1000-2000, included in price of San Lorenzo monastery*, surrounded by lush gardens, and the delightfully frivolous **Casita del Infante** (or the Casita Arriba) ① *same hours as Casita del Príncipe*.

There's a very popular picnic area at the top of the **Monte de la Herrería**, where Felipe II would take a break from his hunting, but you'll probably have to share your spot with coachloads of weekending Madrileños in summer. The tourist office has information on walking trails from the town itself.

Valle de los Caídos (Valley of the Fallen)

① *Tue-Sun Apr-Sep 0930-1900, Oct-Mar 1000-1800; basílica €5, free Wed with EU passport.*
In 1940, work began on a monument to 'the fallen' of the Civil War. Despite the neutral title, its true purpose was the glorification of Franco and his regime and the labourers were Republican prisoners, leftists and anyone who criticized the new government. The setting – a craggy mountain valley with endless views across the plain and down to Madrid – is beautiful, but the monument itself is pompous, overblown and brutally ugly. The vast basilica is built into the rock and topped with an outsized cross (supposedly the largest in the world), visible even from Madrid. Franco is buried by the altar, and the monument has become a focal point for a rally on the anniversary (11 November) of his death.

Sierra de Guadarrama

Since the narrow-gauge railway between Cercedilla and Cotos was opened several decades ago, the Sierra de Guadarrama has become a popular playground for weekending Madrileños, many of whom have second homes here. The Sierra de Guadarrama is not as dramatic or as well known as the Sierra de Gredos to the west, but it's conveniently close to Madrid and offers some spectacular walking, climbing (the peaks of La Maliciosa and La Pedriza) and skiing in winter.

Cercedilla and Cotos The best and most convenient base for hiking in the Sierra de Guadarrama is **Cercedilla**, a rapidly expanding mountain town of chalet-style houses about 70 km from Madrid, which is easily accessible by public transport and stuffed full of bars, shops and restaurants. There's an information centre on the edge of town (just off the main M-966 road from Madrid) which has leaflets describing walking trails around the Valle de la Fuenfría, and is the starting point for a number of excellent hikes.

From here, the narrow gauge railway makes a spectacular journey up to the pretty mountain town of **Cotos**, a small hiking and adventure sports centre. It's about a 20-minute walk from the ski slopes of the Valdesquí resort almost on the border with Segovia.

Navacerrada and around The immaculate village of Navacerrada is another big weekend destination for Madrileños. It has a beautiful mountainous setting on the side of a reservoir, and there are a couple of attractive churches and a buzzy little town square, with a handful of terrace bars and restaurants. But the main attraction is the network of walking trails which lead up into the mountains. Many are found around the small ski resort **Puerto de Navacerrada**, on the road to **Manzanares La Real**, another modest village. It's set on a lake and backed by impressive jagged peaks, but the new housing developments detract from the charm of the old village, with its pretty square and church. There's only one sight: a stubby much-renovated 15th-century castle, which is now a small ethnographical museum, but the views from the top of the keep are wonderful.

Buitrago de Lozoya In the northern reaches of the Sierra de Guadarrama, the attractive town of Buitrago de Lozoya still retains a battered fortress and the defensive walls built by the Moors in the 12th century. During the 15th and 16th centuries, noble families built mansions and fine bridges and the town retains the slightly haughty air of a dowager down on her luck. Look out for the handsome Mudéjar **church of Santa María**, and the unexpected collection of Picasso-related memorabilia in the town hall. The collection was donated by Eugenio Arias, a local barber, and charts his friendship with Picasso with a series of autographed sketches, lithographs, ceramics and postcards. Buitrago is a good starting point for some excellent hikes in the hills and forests of the northern sierra, and the nearby reservoir is good for a swim on a hot summer's day.

Segovia and around → *Phone code: 921. Population: 54,844. For listings, see pages 98-105.*

Segovia is one of the most alluring cities in central Spain, built of golden stone, capped with a fairytale castle and set against the dramatic peaks of the Sierra de Guadarrama. It's almost as famous for its sturdy Castillian cuisine as it is for the enormous Roman aqueduct which has stood here for two millennia. It's the perfect place to relax (although perhaps not at weekends when everyone else is here doing it too) and, if you decide to spend more than the day here, there are gentle walks along the river Eresma, or tougher treks among the surrounding peaks. Close by are two royal residences: the extravagant Bourbon summer palace of La Granja, and the more modest hunting lodge of Riofrío.

Arriving in Segovia
Getting there and around There are regular buses and trains from Madrid. Segovia station is about 2 km from the town centre; take local bus No 3 from outside the station. Most of the sights are clustered in the old city, which is easy to get around on foot. ‣‣ *See Transport, page 104.*

Best time to visit Segovia is especially lovely in early spring, when there's still a slight chill in the air and the mountains are still capped with snow. It can get a little crowded at weekends, particularly during summer, so come off season or during the week if possible.

Tourist information ① *Plaza Azoguejo 1, T921 466 720, www.turismodesegovia.com; regional tourist office at Plaza Mayor 10, T921 460 334.*

Background

Segóbriga was an important military settlement when the Romans built their enormous aqueduct 2000 years ago. In the early Middle Ages, the Arabs introduced the cloth-manufacturing trade, which would ensure Segovia's prosperity long after the Reconquista. Segovia was doing very nicely when Carlos I (Charles V) tried to impose harsh taxes, and revolted. The uprising, known as the Comunero Revolt, was viciously put down and the leaders decapitated in Segovia. Like most of Spain, the city declined in the 18th century when an endless series of wars began. It became popular with tourists in the 20th century, and is also a culinary capital known for its traditional Castilian cuisine.

Segovia

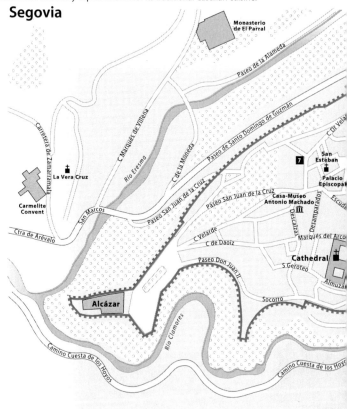

100 metres
100 yards

Where to stay 🛏
Camping Acueducto 1
Hostal Don Jaime 3
Hostal Fornos 4
Hostal Juan Bravo 5

Hostal Plaza 2
Hostería Ayala
Berganza 10
Infanta Isabel 6
Los Linajes 7

Las Sirenas 8
Parador de Segovia 9

Restaurants 🍴
Casa Duque 1

Places in Segovia

The Aqueduct Segovia's most famous sight is at its most dramatic just outside the city walls on Plaza Azoguejo. Nothing holds together the 25,000 stones of this soaring two-storey 760-m-long aqueduct, arching a giddy 29 m high. The tallest surviving Roman aqueduct, it still carried water to the city until a 100 years ago, but pollution and traffic have taken their toll.

Plaza Azoguejo to Plaza Mayor From the Plaza Azoguejo, at the foot of the aqueduct, the busy shop-lined **Calle Cervantes** leads up into the centre of the old city. At the point where it

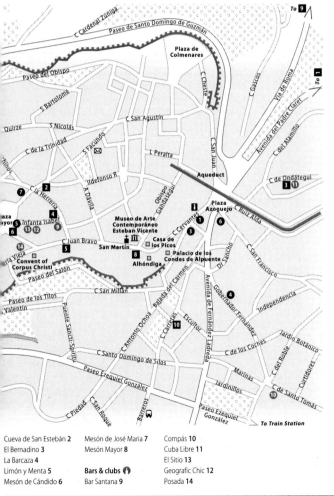

Cueva de San Esteban **2**
El Bernadino **3**
La Barcaza **4**
Limón y Menta **5**
Mesón de Cándido **6**

Mesón de José Maria **7**
Mesón Mayor **8**

Bars & clubs 🎵
Bar Santana **9**

Compás **10**
Cuba Libre **11**
El Sitio **13**
Geografic Chic **12**
Posada **14**

turns across the old city walls, you can't miss the knobbly 15th-century **Casa de los Picos** (House of the Spikes), which got everyone talking when it was first built thanks to its unusual façade of diamond-shaped jutting stones. It's now a cultural and exhibition centre, and you can step in to admire the graceful patio. The elegant mansion covered in swirling *esgrafado* tucked away close by is the **Palacio de los Condes de Alpuente**, and below it is the former corn exchange (**Alhondiga**), a Gothic building with an Arabic name which was built under the Catholic Kings. Continuing along Calle de Cervantes, the softly rounded Romanesque church of **San Martín**, with its covered portico and Mudéjar belltower, overlooks a peaceful square with a statue of Juan Bravo, the leader of the Comunero Revolt (with a name like that, he was bound to be a folk hero).

Close by is one of Segovia's newest museums, the **Museo de Arte Contemporáneo Esteban Vicente** ① *Plaza de Bellas Artes, T921 462 010, www.museoestebanvicente.es, Tue-Sat 1100-14000 and 1600-1900, Sun 1100-1400; €3/€1.50*, devoted to the Segovian painter Esteban Vicente (1903-2000). He spent most of his life in New York, but made provisions in his will for his art to be returned to his native city and his vivid paintings are now housed in the handsomely restored 15th-century Palacio de Enrique IV.

Calle Juan Bravo links Plaza San Martín with old Segovia's main square, the wide appealing **Plaza Mayor**, full of terrace bars/restaurants and the heart of the city's nightlife. There's a small bandstand in the centre, where concerts are occasionally held in summer.

Cathedral ① *Apr-Sep 0930-1830, Oct Mar 0930-1730, museum closed Sun morning, €3/€2.* Rising serenely above the Plaza Mayor, Segovia's cathedral was built between 1525 and 1590 in what is probably the latest example of the Gothic style in Spain. The original cathedral was destroyed by Carlos I (Charles V) during his vicious repression of the Comunero Revolt (see Background, above), but he must have had a guilty conscience because he provided the funds for a replacement. Designed by Juan Gil de Hontañón, it is fashionably austere in the way the Spanish liked their churches in those days, but the soft golden stone of the exterior manages to counteract its harshness. Inside there is some elegant vaulting in the chapels surrounding the ambulatory, but little else to see. The cloister was all that remained of the original cathedral and was brought here brick by brick. Just off the cloister is the Sala Capitular, where the cathedral's scant treasures are gathered; just a few gold and silver religious ornaments, some fine 17th-century tapestries, and a curious, but rather pretty, painted 16th-century English clock.

Around the Cathedral Many of the most important religious buildings connected to the cathedral are set around the Plaza de San Esteban, just northeast of the Plaza Mayor. A magnificent, six-storey Italianate tower looms above the delicate **church of San Esteban**, with a striking Crucifixion inside. Nearby, the **Palacio Episcopal** (Episcopal Palace) ① *closed for renovation; check hours with the tourist office*, was given a florid 18th-century makeover but retains its curious Renaissance façade – more interesting that the old-fashioned museum of religious paintings and statuary inside.

Between 1919 and 1932 the poet **Antonio Machado** stayed in a boarding house on Callejuela de los Desamparados (just off the Plaza de San Esteban), which has been transformed into a engaging little **museum** ① *Wed-Sun 1100-1400, 1000-1830, €2, free on Wed*, dedicated to his life and work.

The **Judería**, once home to a Jewish community before the expulsion of the Jews, sits behind the cathedral to the south. It's a slightly run-down neighbourhood now, but the crooked passages and leaning houses make it quietly atmospheric. The former synagogue (the best preserved of the five that the city once boasted) is now part of the **Convent of Corpus Christi** ⓘ *Plaza del Corpus, T921 463 429, call in advance for opening times*, and although much of it is a 19th-century recreation after fire destroyed the original building, it's worth a visit for the glimpse it gives into life in the Jewish community. The **Centro Didáctico de la Judería** ⓘ *C/Judería Vieja 12, T921 462 396, daily 1000-1400, 1600-1900, €2*, was the former home of Abraham Senneor, and later of Andrés Laguna, the king's physician. It relates the history of Segovia's Jewish community.

Alcázar ⓘ *Plaza de la Reina Victoria Eugenia, T921 460 759, www.alcazardesegovia.com, Oct-Mar 1000-1800, Apr-Sep 1000-1900, €4.50, free 3rd Tue of every month.* Segovia's Alcázar sits on a cliff edge, bristling with storybook turrets and spires. Purists sniff that the current version, a fanciful 19th-century restoration, bears no resemblance to the original, but Disney apparently liked it so much they used it as a model for their first theme park. The first fortress on this site was built in the 12th century, in order to protect newly reconquered Segovia. It was a favourite with Castilian monarchs during the Middle Ages, but when Madrid was appointed the permanent capital of the court, it fell out of favour. No longer used as a palace, it became a prison and military school and was almost completely destroyed by fire in 1862. The interior has been fitted out with armour and weapons, but the real highlights are the spectacular *artesonado* ceilings which glitter magnificently in almost every room. A useful plan and explanatory leaflet (which remains coy on the issue of what's authentic and what's not) is included in the admission price. There's a 144-step hike up the old watchtower for stupendous views out across the lovely old city to the mountains, still snow-capped in late spring.

Outside the city walls Segovia is stuffed full of beautiful churches. One of the loveliest, the little 13th-century **Iglesia de la Vera Cruz** (Church of the True Cross), is also built with Segovia's warm, honey-coloured stone, and sits just outside the city walls. It's constructed on a polygonal plan typical of Templar churches, and the double-chamber at its heart was used for the Order's secret rituals. Its fortunes have declined in the past few centuries and even the sliver of the True Cross which gave it its name has gone to another local church. Don't miss the fabulous views across Segovia from the **belltower** ⓘ *Apr-Sep Tue 1600-1900, Wed-Sun 1030-1330 and 1600-1900; Oct-Mar Tue 1600-1800, Wed-Sun 1030-1330 and 1600-1800, €2, free Tue afternoon.*

The remains of Saint John of the Cross are buried in an elaborate early 20th-century mausoleum in the nearby Carmelite **convent** ⓘ *Mon 1530-1800, Tue-Sun 1000-1330 and 1600-1900, until 2000 in summer, free but donations welcome,* hidden behind massive walls.

Segovia has some excellent gentle walking and you can take a peaceful stroll through the valley of the Río Eresma to the luminous **Monasterio de El Parral** ⓘ *C/del Marqués de Villena, T921 431 298, visits Sat, Sun and public holidays 1000, 1130, 1615, 1745, free but donations accepted.* The quiet church contains the alabaster tombs of the Villena family and a fine 16th-century retablo, a beautiful backdrop to Mass held in Gregorian chant on Sundays at midday, and during the week at 1300.

Around Segovia
ⓘ *www.patrimonionacional.es, both palaces open Apr-Sep Tue-Sun 1000-1800, Oct-Mar Tue-Sun 1000-2000, €9, valid 48 hrs for both palaces, free on Wed (Oct-Mar 1500-1800; Apr-Sep 1700-2000) and to EU passport holders.*

There are two sumptuous royal palaces close to Segovia; **La Granja de San Ildefonso** is a 10-minute bus ride away, but you'll need your own transport to get to the former hunting lodge at **Ríofrío**. La Granja, a frothy Italian-style palace built for the Bourbon monarchs, is surrounded by magnificent gardens, famous for their fountains and sculptures. Unfortunately, you can only see the fountains in all their glory on three days a year, normally 30 May, 25 July and 25 August (they turn on a few on Wednesdays and weekends at 1730 to whet your appetite). The palace was destroyed by fire in 1918, but it has been carefully restored and the royal apartments are now a magnificent evocation of the opulence of the 18th-century Spanish court. Entry to the adjoining **Museo de Tapices** (Tapestry Museum) and the Collegiata (where Felipe V and his wife and son are buried surrounded by a macabre collection of relics and old bones) are both included in the ticket price. If you've been dazzled by the gorgeous crystal chandeliers, you can find out how they were made at the museum set in the former **Real Fábrica de Cristales** (Royal Crystal Factory).

The palace at Ríofrío is difficult to get to without your own transport, and is much lower key. It is beautifully set among forests and woods and attracts considerably fewer visitors than La Granja, which can be a charm in itself. Despite its grand scale, Ríofrío was merely a hunting lodge, and now half of it has been given up to a bizarre museum of hunting, complete with row upon row of stuffed heads. It's surrounded by a deer park (inaccessible on foot, although you can drive through it).

Ávila → *Phone code: 920. Population: 58,900. Altitude: 1,128 m. For listings, see pages 98-105.*

The austere mountain town of Ávila is set on a windswept plateau, surrounded by the chilly granite peaks of the Sierra de Gredos. The reddish-brown tangle of medieval mansions and Romanesque churches is completely enclosed by magnificent medieval walls, studded with towers and crenellations. This 'city of saints and stones' is the birthplace of Santa Teresa, the 16th-century mystic, visionary and writer, and is still a major pilgrimage centre. It remains a hushed and contemplative city but, if it all gets too much, you can easily escape to the surrounding mountains, scattered with attractive old villages, and a paradise for hikers and climbers. While you are here, try some *yemas*, a delicious sticky sweet made of egg yolk and sugar, traditionally made by Ávila's nuns.

Arriving in Ávila
Getting there and around There are regular bus and train connections with Madrid, Salamanca and Segovia, as well as other major cities in Castilla y León. The old walled city of Ávila is small and easy to get around on foot. → *See Transport, page 104.*

Best time to visit Late spring and early autumn are the best times to visit Ávila and the Sierra de Gredos, when the temperatures are mild and the streets and hiking trails empty. The city is chilly in winter, although the surrounding mountains are especially beautiful covered in snow. For the very best views of the walls themselves, head to the little shrine at Cuatro Postes just outside town on the Salamanca road.

Tourist information ① *Av Madrid 39, T920 225 969, www.avilaturismo.com.* The tourist office has an excellent leaflet describing a walk around the old city which takes in the best of the palaces.

Something in the air

Teresa de Cepada y Ahumada was born to an aristocratic family on 28 March 1515. At the age of seven she ran away to be martyred by the Moors (her family caught up with her just outside town, and a small stone cross marks the spot) and then joined the Carmelites at the age of 18. More than 20 years passed before she had the first of her famous visions, in which an angel pierced her heart with flaming arrows. In the second, the Virgin instructed her to remove her shoes and reform the Carmelite order, which had drifted away from its original vows of poverty and simplicity. Teresa embarked on a journey around Spain, urging reform and founding the Discalced – 'shoeless' – Carmelites, but her success aroused jealousy and suspicion within the Church. She and her confessor, Juan de Yepes, were both imprisoned in Toledo, where Teresa wrote *The Inner Castle*, a classic mystical text describing the journey of a Bride of Christ, and Juan wrote the poetic *Dark Night of the Soul*. Teresa died in 1582 when her writings were still regarded with suspicion by the Church, who then did a strange about-face and canonised her in 1622. Juan de Yepes died miserably, persecuted to the last, but was also canonised as Saint John of the Cross in 1726.

Teresa and Juan were not the only spiritual writers to emerge from the city. The 13th-century Jewish cleric Mose Ben Shemthom, author of the *Book of Splendour* (*Seger-ha-Zohar*) one of the most important Hebraic texts, was also from Ávila, and Mancebo de Arévalo's *Tafçira* was one of the last Islamic spiritual texts to come out of Spain before the expulsion of the Moors.

Background

According to legend, Ávila was founded by Hercules himself. The famous walls were initiated under Alfonso VI in the 11th century, when the city was in the front line of the Reconquista. And yet Ávila was famous for its learning and religious tolerance, and the city never really recovered economically after the expulsion of the Jews in 1492 and then the Moriscos in 1609. In the 16th century, the city produced two outstanding religious figures: Teresa of Ávila and St John of the Cross, who were canonized and subsequently declared Doctors of the Church. The cult of Saint Teresa, in particular, is still very strong and she is co-patron saint of Spain (see box, above).

Places in Ávila

Muralla de Ávila ① *Entrance at Puerta del Puente, C/Marqués de Santo Domingo s/n, T920 354 000, http://muralladeavila.com, Tue-Sun Apr-mid Oct 1000-2000, mid Oct-Mar 1100-1800, €5/€3.50*. A visit to the city should begin at Ávila's famous **walls**. Constructed in the wake of Alfonse VI's victory in Toledo, these massive walls were erected to ensure that the Arab armies couldn't recapture the city. Some 12 m high, 3 m thick, and studded with nine gates and 88 towers, they became legendary. A short section has been made into a panoramic walkway, with views out over the old city, and up to the peaks of the Sierra de Gredos.

Cathedral and around ① *Plaza de Catedral, T920 211 641, Nov-Mar Mon-Fri 1000-1700, Sat 1000-1800, Sun 1200-1700, Apr-Oct Mon-Fri 1000-1800, Sat 1000-1900, Sun 1200-1700, €4/€3.50*. As the massive city walls were being erected to defend the city from the Moors, the cathedral was slowly rising to take its place in the struggle for souls. It was incorporated into the walls to become a literal and metaphorical bastion, and the austere façade betrays its dual function as a fortress and place of worship. The interior is surprisingly lovely, with its lofty Gothic nave made of rosy stone, and magnificent Plateresque stalls and retrochoir all gently illuminated by stained glass windows. One of Ávila's most famous medieval bishops is buried in an extravagant alabaster sarcophagus behind the altar; his dark skin earned him the nickname 'El Tostado' – 'the toasted'. The cloister, attractively rumpled and overgrown, is home to several storks' nests; just off it is the cathedral museum, with a rather disappointing collection of paintings, religious ornaments (including Juan de Arfe's massive Monstrance) and vestments.

Ávila once contained so many aristocratic palaces that it was known as 'City of the Nobles'. One of the grandest, the 16th-century **Casa de los Velada** (now a hotel), which overlooks the Plaza de la Catedral, has lodged Carlos I (Charles V), Isabel la Católica and Felipe II. Opposite the cathedral, C/de los Reyes Católicos leads to the **Plaza del Mercado Chico**, originally the site of the Roman forum and still the heart of the old city. It's flanked on one side by the 19th-century Ayuntamiento (Town Hall) and on the other by the church of **San Juan**, where Santa Teresa was baptised. The font has been preserved and the church can be visited before and after Mass.

Ávila

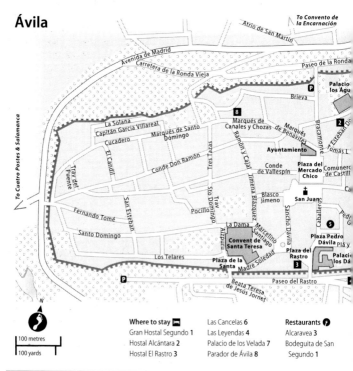

Where to stay 🛏	Las Cancelas 6	Restaurants 🍴
Gran Hostal Segundo 1	Las Leyendas 4	Alcaravea 3
Hostal Alcántara 2	Palacio de los Velada 7	Bodeguita de San
Hostal El Rastro 3	Parador de Ávila 8	Segundo 1

Convento de Santa Teresa ① *Plaza de la Santa, T920 211 030, Apr-Oct Tue-Sun 1000-1400 and 1600-1900, Nov-Mar 1000-1330 and 1530-1730, €3/€1.50.* Also known as the Convento de la Santa, this convent was founded in 1636 on the site of the Cepeda mansion where Teresa of Ávila was born. The Baroque convent contains a flamboyant chapel to Saint Teresa, and several statues by Gregorio Fernández. A **museum** devoted to the life of the saint has been established around the corner on Calle La Dama; the setting, a stone cellar, is attractive, but the exhibits are extremely dull. There are plenty of dire portraits of the saint, a few old documents, a reproduction of her cell, and a collection of her works in different languages. The most interesting section is at the end, where 'before' and 'after' (as in 'before taking Holy Orders') photographs of more recent Carmelite saints are displayed, including one of Edith Stein (later Santa Teresa Benedicta de la Cruz) who died in Auschwitz.

More mansions Old Ávila is a strange little time capsule, with a rich collection of noble mansions and churches that have survived through neglect rather than any concerted efforts at preservation. Most of its modern inhabitants live in the convenient new housing developments outside the city walls, leaving the quiet streets of the old town to pilgrims and visitors. Many of the best surviving mansions (all private) are concentrated on the southern side of the city, including the elaborate palace-fortress of the **Dávila** on Calle de Cepadas, which incorporates four houses dating back to the 13th century. There is another clutch of palaces in the northeastern corner of the city; look out for the **Mansión de los Verdugo** and the nearby **Palacio de los Águila**, on Calle López Nuñez, both typically fortified aristocratic palaces with a wealth of elaborate Renaissance detailing.

Outside the city walls Many of Ávila's finest churches are located just outside the city walls; one of the oldest is the simple Romanesque **Iglesia de San Pedro** which overlooks the arcaded **Plaza de Santa Teresa** (known locally as the Plaza Grande). It's a handsome, bustling square edged with arcades containing plenty of shops and bars. The **Museo Provincial** ① *Plaza de los Nalvillos 3, T920 211 003; Jul-Sep Tue-Sat 1000-1400 and 1700-2000, Sun 1000-1400; Oct-Jun Tue-Sat 1000-1400 and 1600-1900, Sun 1000-1400; €1.20, free on Sat and Sun,* is held in the Palacio de los Deanes and the nearby Romanesque church of Santo Tomé el Viejo, just off the Plaza de Italia, and contains an odd but appealing assortment of ceramics, archaeological findings, religious art and traditional costumes and furnishings.

Casa Patas 2
Fogón de Santa Teresa 4
La Casona 5

The finest Romanesque church in Ávila is the **Basílica de San Vicente**, to the north of the museum on the Paseo Humilladero. San Vicente's life and martyrdom is depicted in grisly detail on a 12th-century sepulchre, and the subterranean crypt contains the slab on which he, along with his two sisters, was martyred at the hands of the Romans. The crypt is also an important stop on the pilgrimage trail, as it was here that Saint Teresa had the second of her visions and where, according to tradition, she took off her shoes in answer to the Virgin's request for reform of the Carmelite order. Teresa spent almost 30 years in the **Convento de la Encarnación** ① *C/Encarnación, T920 211 212, Tue-Fri 0930-1330 and 1530-1800, Sat 1000-1300 and 1600-1800, €2/€1.50*, which now contains a small museum of her life.

The most important monument outside the city walls is the Dominican **Monasterio Réal de Santo Tomás** ① *T920 352 237, www.monasteriosantotomas.es, 1000-1400 and 1530-1930, free entry into the church, €4/€3 to visit cloisters and choir*, a good 15-minute walk from the old city. It's set around three cloisters and was established at the end of the 15th century by the Catholic kings. It did service as their summer residence, and was also the seat of Ávila's university. But its glory days have long gone, and grass sprouts through the cracks in the paving stones of the first and smallest cloister, the Cloister of the Noviciate. The second cloister, the Cloister of Silence, is larger, grander, and handsomely decorated with engravings on the upper gallery. The third and grandest cloister is the Cloister of the Kings, but it's also the least atmospheric. Back in the Cloister of Silence, a small staircase leads up to an exquisitely carved Gothic choir which gives a beautiful bird's-eye-view of the elegant Gothic church. The sumptuous alabaster tomb behind the main altar belongs to Don Juan, the only son of the Catholic kings. His premature death had far-reaching consequences for the country, and the Catholic kings were succeeded by Carlos I (Charles V), Spain's first Habsburg ruler. Torquemada, the notorious inquisitor, is buried in the Sacristy.

Sierra de Gredos → *For listings, see pages 98-105*.

The Sierra de Gredos is the westernmost region of the Sistema Central, the spiky range which, with the Sierra de Guadarrama, forms Spain's craggy backbone. It's a beautiful region of forested peaks and stone villages, and it offers excellent opportunities for hiking, fishing, hang-gliding, horse riding, mountain biking and other sports. Not surprisingly, it has become a popular refuge for stressed-out city-dwellers who have bought up holiday homes, but there's still not a great deal of accommodation in the region and it's worth checking out the *casas rurales* (see below).

Arriving in Sierra de Gredos
Getting there and around Public transport is restricted to sporadic and infrequent services from Madrid and Ávila, so consider renting a car.

Tourist information There is no visitor centre within the limits of the Parque Regional de la Sierra de Gredos. There are lists of *casas rurales* online at www.casasgredos.com. Local tourist information offices have some details of walking routes, but you should pick up detailed walking guides and maps in advance from bookshops in Madrid or Ávila.

Arenas de San Pedro

Arenas de San Pedro is one of the largest and most accessible towns in the region, a popular weekend retreat crammed with craft shops and second homes. Sights include the sturdy 15th-century **Castillo de la Triste Condessa** (Castle of the Sad Countess), named for the unfortunate Juana Pimental who was beheaded by Juan II of Castille, a **Gothic church** which contains the tomb of San Pedro de Alcántara who died here in 1562, and the simple **Puente Romano** (which is actually medieval). Its most famous sight is the **Cueva del Águila**, 10 km from the village, which is filled with stalagmites and stalactites. There is a traditional pilgrimage to the **Santuario de San Pedro**, 3 km from the town, in mid-October when the local festival is celebrated with bullfights and plenty of carousing on the streets. The **tourist office** ① *Plaza de San Pedro s/n, T920 370 245, http://arenasdesanpedro.es*, has details of walking routes throughout the Sierra, but the string of delightful tiny villages – **Guisando**, **El Arenal**, and particularly **El Hornillo** – a few kilometres north of Arenas make better bases for hikers, with several routes splintering off into the mountains.

Hoyos del Espino and Navarredonda de Gredos

These unassuming villages have a spectacular setting in the northern foothills of the Sierra de Gredos, and are good bases for circular walks. A 12-km asphalt road leads from Hoyos (there's another from Navarredonda) to the **Plataforma de Gredos**. From here, it's a spectacular two-hour trek on a well-marked reasonably easy path to the **Laguna Grande** (there's a *refugio* here where you can sleep and eat, T920 207 576/T918 476 253, www.refugiodelola.com) in the **Circo de Gredos** at the centre of the park. The lake, a glowing, unearthly emerald, reflects the granite bulk of the **Pico del Almanzor** (2593 m), the highest peak of the Sierra de Gredos. There are tourist offices in Navarredonda (Plaza de Calvo Sotelo 1, T920 345 252) and Hoyos (Cruce de la Ctra de la Plataforma de Gredos, T920 349 035).

Piedrahíta and El Barco de Ávila

Piedrahíta, 60 km southwest of Ávila, is a handsome town with a smattering of noble mansions and a porticoed main square. The 18th-century **Palacio de los Duques de Alba** is surrounded by gardens designed in imitation of those at La Granja (see page 82), although they are not as manicured or well kept. The nearby **Puerta de la Peña Negra** is popular with hang-gliders from all over Spain. Piedrahíta's **tourist office** ① *Plaza de España, T920 360 001*, is in the Ayuntamiento.

Some 20 km further west, heading towards the Valle de la Vera in Extremadura, is El Barco de Ávila, one of the loveliest towns in the region, with an incomparable setting on the edge of the Sierra de Gredos and overlooked by a ruined castle. It also has a fine Plaza Mayor – officially the Plaza de España – and a serene Gothic church with a pretty belltower. El Barco de Ávila's **tourist office** ① *Plaza de España 4, T920 340 888*, is only open in July and August .

Alcalá de Henares and around → *For listings, see pages 98-105.*

An engaging, quietly affluent city, Alcalá de Henares is scattered with plenty of opulent reminders of the glory days of the 16th and 17th centuries. Set 35 km east of Madrid (on the main motorway route to Zaragoza), it's an easy day trip from the capital but, if you've got more time, you could make a diversion to the unusual 18th-century planned town of **Nuevo Báztan**. For information contact the **tourist office** ① *Plaza de Cervantes, T918 892 694, www.turismoalcala.es.*

Background

Alcalá de Henares' claim to fame was its university, which was established by Cardinal Cisneros (confessor to Isabel II) in 1498, and which came to rival even that of Salamanca as the intellectual centre of Spain. Named the Complutense after the Roman name for the town, Complutum, the university produced the world's first polyglot bible (you can see an example of it in the Ayuntamiento/town hall) but it's most famous as the birthplace of Cervantes. He wasn't the only famous resident: Calderón de la Barca, Lope de Vega and Ignatius Loyola all studied here during Spain's Golden Age. The university moved to Madrid in the 19th century and the city went into decline – which has been dramatically reversed since the university's return to Alcalá in 1977.

Places in Alcalá de Henares

The centre of Alcalá is the **Plaza de Cervantes**, a long formal square edged with arcaded narrow mansions, and shaded by plane trees. There are plenty of bars and restaurants with tables spilling out on to the square, and a small bandstand for concerts on warm summer nights. Cervantes was baptised in the rosy 15th-century **Capilla del Oidor** that stands at the top of the square, and has a slim, graceful belltower, and the 17th-century **Teatro de Cervantes**, which is believed to be the oldest surviving public theatre in Europe, was discovered under the square in 1980. Now restored, it offers a programme of events each weekend.

Most of the major university buildings are clustered near here, including the striking **Colegio Mayor de San Ildefonso** (1537-1553) ① *Plaza de San Diego, T918 856 487, www.uah.es; ask at the tourist office about guided visits*, which overlooks the Plaza de San Diego just to the east of the Plaza de Cervantes. The spectacular Plateresque façade is the work of Rodrigo Gil de Hontañón, and the well at the centre of the finest of the three internal patios is sculpted with swans (*cisnes*), in a neat reference to Cardinal Cisneros, the founder of the university. Admission is by guided tour only (although you can usually peek into the main patio) and includes entrance to the Parainfo, a sumptuous hall with a magnificent coffered ceiling, where the award ceremony for Spain's most prestigious literary prize, the Premio Cervantes, is held annually on 23 April. The Capilla de San Ildefonso is equally dazzling, a glittering mix of Gothic, Mudéjar and Renaissance styles, with plenty of gleaming white stucco ornamentation and an exquisite coffered ceiling. Many of the university's most influential associates are buried here, including Felipe II's physician, El Divino Vallés, and Antonio de Nebrija. The creamy, ornately carved alabaster tomb of Cardenal Cisneros doesn't actually contain his mortal remains, which were buried instead in the cathedral.

The delightful **Calle Mayor** runs down from the Plaza de Cervantes and is still overhung with crooked medieval houses. Once the main market street of the Judería or Jewish Quarter, it's still lined with the porticoes which would once have sheltered stall-holders and market traders. Now it's become a rather chic shopping area, with plenty of cafés and bars for a break. On the right, Cervantes' birthplace has been converted into a charming museum, **Casa-Museo de Cervantes** ① *Tue-Sun 1000-1800, free.* The house is set around a patio, now glassed over, and contains typical period furnishings, including a recently discovered Renaissance mural in one room. Downstairs are the social and public rooms, including a sturdy Castillian kitchen and a special area for women with a raised platform known as the *estrado de las damas*, a Muslim tradition that found its way into Spanish culture. Upstairs, one room has been devoted to dozens of editions from around the world and across the centuries of Cervantes' famous work, Don Quixote, and there's also a sweet little children's room with toys and books. Cardinal Cisneros is buried in the early 16th-century **cathedral of Saints Just and Pastor**, which commemorates the two child saints who were martyred on this spot according to legend. To the west, the **Archbishop's Palace** dates back to the 13th century and is topped with an untidy fringe of storks' nests. For a glimpse into Alcalá's Roman past, visit the former **Convento de la Madre de Dios** next door, which has been converted into an **archaeology museum** ① *Tue-Sat 1100-1900, Sun and hols 1100-1500, free*, and is largely devoted to the discoveries made in the Roman settlement of Complutum just outside Alcalá.

Around Alcalá de Henares

Nuevo Baztán, 20 km from Alcalá, is a sort of 18th-century Milton Keynes. Juan de Goyeneche commissioned the celebrated Baroque architect José Benito de Churriguera to create a purpose-built town which was to include a palace for himself, a church, and homes and workshops for the community of craftspeople whom he hoped to encourage to live there. He named it after his home village in Navarra. The project attracted a great deal of enthusiasm at the beginning but it wasn't long before the excitement fizzled out; everything looked fabulous but nothing seemed to work. Even the new glass factory, established by Felipe VI, was forced to close because of fuel problems. Nuevo Baztán became a ghost town. You can still visit the palace and church, built as a single unit and the centrepiece of Nuevo Baztán, but much of it is now sadly dilapidated.

Aranjuez → *For listings, see pages 98-105.*

Lush Aranjuez, about 45 km southeast of Madrid, is a rare oasis of green in the sun-baked Castillian plain. It's famous throughout Spain for its asparagus and strawberries, and is a very popular weekend outing for Madrileño families. To get there in style, take the 'Strawberry Train' ('Tren de la Fresa'), a steam train which departs from the train museum in Madrid (see page 47).

Places in Aranjuez

The Bourbons built an extravagant Versailles-inspired **palace** ① *Oct-Mar 1000-1800, Apr-Sep 1000-2000, €9/€4 (guided visit plus €6, audioguide plus €4), free to EU-passport holders on Wed*, to escape Madrid's searing summer heat, and surrounded it with spectacular gardens. Destroyed by fire in 1727, it had barely been rebuilt before another fire ripped through it in 1748. It has been beautifully restored and filled with original furniture and vast crystal chandeliers; highlights include the spectacular Salón de Baile, an enormous ballroom with wonderful views of the gardens, and the Salón de Porcelana, in which every inch is encrusted with porcelain chinoiserie in the purest rococo style. The dramatic throne room has blood red velvet walls and an elaborate allegory of the monarchy on the ceiling. Downstairs, the quirky **Museo de La Vida** has a motley collection of fans, military uniforms, kitchen utensils and all kinds of other odds and ends. Best of all is the bizarre early portable gym, and the collection of toys which includes a mini-Hansom cab, a tiny bicycle with an enormous front wheel, a doll's house and miniature uniforms and guns.

Aranjuez is most famous for its exquisite **gardens** ① *Oct-Mar 0800-1830, Apr-Sep 0800-2030, free*, which provide delightful relief from the scorching summer heat. Behind the palace are the manicured, elegant Jardines de la Isla and the Parterre, which combine elements of Italian, French, Dutch and Islamic garden design. The most extensive gardens are the **Jardínes de la Princípe**, vast, cool and shady, which stretch along the river bank. At the furthest end of these gardens, Carlos IV's whimsical summer pavilion, the **Casa del Labrador** ① *T918 910 305, same hours as palace, included in palace ticket*, is now a delightful museum and perhaps even more opulent than the royal palace itself. Stuffed full of silken tapestries, fine porcelain, ornate clocks, Roman statuary, and paintings, a tour through the sumptuous apartments is a dizzying experience – and as far from the home of an ordinary labourer (*labrador*) as one could possibly get.

Down by the river, the royal boathouse has been converted into a fascinating little museum of royal barges, the **Museu de Falúas Reales** ① *Jardínes del Príncipe, same hours as palace, included in palace ticket*. Gawp at the ornate craft used to transport languid Royals downriver, from the gorgeous 17th-century Venetian barge covered with gilded nymphs and garlands, to Isabel II's sumptuous barge inlaid with mahogany and gold silk. For further information contact the **tourist office** ① *Plaza de San Antonio 9, T918 910 427*.

Chinchón → *For listings, see pages 98-105.*

Chinchón, a charming hill town about 50 km southeast of Madrid, is set around a famously lovely Plaza Mayor. So famous, in fact, that your chances of getting a table at one of the square's equally famous *mesónes* on a Sunday, are virtually nil. Even Orson Welles fell under Chinchón's spell, and filmed parts of *Chimes At Midnight* and *An Immortal Story* here. The dramatic connection is apt; the square is a perfectly preserved example of an early *corral de la comedias*, an outdoor theatre which was also used for bullfights, hangings, and markets and all manner of public entertainment. The elegant tiers of wooden galleries still offer a perfect view of the action below during local fiestas when *corridas* are still held. Chinchón is also known for the production of *anís*, a pungent aniseed-flavoured liqueur, which you can buy from the scores of distilleries and souvenir shops that dot the town. Better yet, come for the annual **Fiesta del Anís y Vino** in mid-April (if you don't mind the crowds) when you can sample the stuff to your heart's content. The town is also known for the Easter passion plays, enacted by the locals. Chinchón's **tourist office** ① *Plaza Mayor 6, T918 935 323, www.ciudad-chinchon.com*, is in the town hall.

Toledo → *Phone code: 925. Population: 84,019. Altitude: 529 m. For listings, see pages 98-105.*

Toledo was an captivating city of shadowy streets, sitting on a hilltop above the River Tajo and less than an hour's drive from Madrid. Famously one of the most learned and tolerant cities of medieval Spain, its once-glorious past is recalled in the magnificent palaces, mansions and churches that cram the maze of narrow passages. Unsurprisingly, then, it's also a tourist honeypot, stuffed full of coaches, souvenir shops, and restaurants with laminated menus in a dozen languages. Come in the off-season, or stay overnight if you can: when the day-trippers are gone and quiet falls on the ancient town, it remains one of the most beguiling cities in Spain.

Arriving in Toledo
Getting there and around Toledo is served by regular trains and buses from Madrid. The train station is a gorgeous neo-Mudéjar fantasy, about a 20-minute walk from the city centre. The bus station is about 10 minutes. Take bus No 5 or 6 to get to the Plaza de Zocodovar in the city centre from the train station. There are several local bus services from the bus station. Once you've made it inside the walls, you can walk everywhere – Toledo's narrow streets were not designed for cars or buses. ▸▸ *See Transport, page 105.*

Orientation The old walled city sits on the top of a hill in a loop in the River Tajo, with the newer neighbourhoods spreading out beyond the walls. Once in the maze of streets of the *casco histórico*, you will certainly get lost (enjoy it, everyone does) but somehow all streets seem to lead back to the massive cathedral in the centre.

Best time to visit The religious processions for Corpus Christi are famous throughout Spain. It is heaving in summer – spring and autumn are best for escaping the crowds.

Tourist information ⓘ *Puerta de Bisagra s/n, T925 220 843, www.turismocastillala mancha.com, Mon-Fri 1000-1800, Sat 0900-1900, Sun and hols 0900-1500. Ayuntamiento, Plaza de Ayuntamiento, T925 254 030, www.toledo-turismo.com, Mon 1030-1430, Tue-Sun 1030-1430 and 1630-1900.*

Background
Toledo has been an important settlement long before the Romans conquered it in the second century BC, and succeeding waves of conquerors and settlers have all left their mark here. During the Middle Ages, it gained a formidable reputation for learning and religious tolerance, and Muslims, Jews and Christians lived together in comparative harmony: after the Reconquest, Toledo's new ruler Alfonso VI gave himself the title 'Emperor of the Three Religions'. Cultured, prosperous Toledo was in the running for capital, but when Madrid won the race in 1561, it lost most of its influence and became a quiet backwater. El Greco retired here after refusing to butter up his royal patrons in Madrid, and the city holds an extensive collection of his works. Always in the shadow of Madrid, it wasn't until the Civil War that Toledo re-entered the history books with the famous Siege of the Alcázar in 1936, when more than a thousand Nationalist soldiers and their families held out while the fortress was bombed to smithereens around them.

Toledo

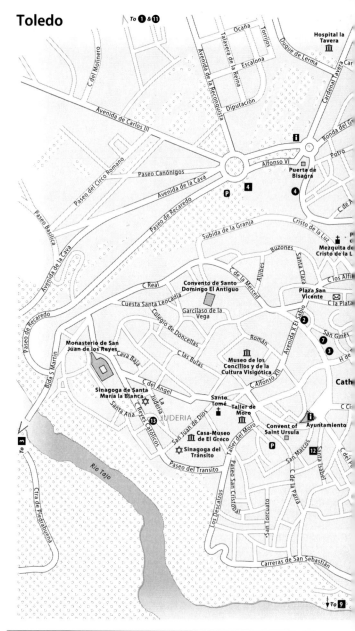

To ① & ⑪

Ocaña

Hospital la
Tavera
🏛

Talavera de la Reina
Torrijos
Duque de Lerma
Cardenal Tavera
Car

Avenida de la Reconquista
Escalona
Diputación

Avenida de Carlos III

Ronda del G

C del Molinero

Paseo del Circo Romano
Paseo Canónigos
Avenida de la Cava
Avenida de Recaredo
Alfonso VI
Puerta de
Bisagra
❹
❹

Potro

C de A

Paseo Basílica
Paseo de Recaredo
P
❹

Cristo de la Luz

Subida de la Granja

Buzones

Mezquita de
Cristo de la L

Avenida de la Cava

C Real
Convento de Santo
Domingo El Antiguo
C de la Merced
Aljibes
Santa Clara
Plaza San
Vicente
C los Alfi
C la Plata

Cuesta Santa Leocadia
Garcilaso de la
Vega
Colegio de Doncellas
Avenida X El Salvo
❷
San Ginés
❼
❸
H de

Paseo de Recaredo

Monasterio de San
Juan de los Reyes
Cava Baja
C las Bulas
Román
Museo de los
Concilios y de la
Cultura Visigótica
🏛
Alfonso XI

Cath

Bda S Martín

Sinagoga de Santa
María la Blanca
✡
C del Angel
La Judería
Santa Ana
Reyes Católicos
JUDERIA
❸
Santo
Tomé
Taller de
Moro
🏛

C Cis

Convent of
Saint Ursula
🏛
Ayuntamiento
🛈

To ❸
San Juan de Dios
Casa-Museo
de El Greco
🏛
Sinagoga del
Tránsito
✡
Taller del Moro
Paseo San Cristóbal
P
San Marcos
❿
Santa Isabel
del P

Paseo del Transito

Río Tajo

Ctra de Piedrabuena
Los Descalzos
C de la patra
San Torcuato

Carreras de San Sebastián

↓ To ❾

N

| 100 metres |
| 100 yards |

Where to stay 🛏

Albergue Juvenil **1**
Alfonso VI **2**
Camping El Greco **3**
Hostal Cardenal **4**
Hostal Centro **5**
Hostal Madrid **6**
La Almunia **7**
La Posada de Manolo **8**
Parador Conde
  de Orgaz **9**
Pensión Castilla **10**
Santa Isabel **12**

Restaurants 🍴

Albaicín **1**
Asador Adolfo **3**
Casa Ludeña **5**
Casón de los López
  de Toledo **6**
Cervecería Adolfo **7**
El Trébol **8**
La Abadía **10**
La Cepa Andaluza **11**
La Flor de la Esquina **2**
La Perdiz **13**
La Virgen de la Estrella **4**
Mille Grazie **16**

Bars & clubs 🍸

El Último **17**

Places in Toledo

Catedral de Toledo ① *C/Cardenal Cisneros s/n, T925 222 241, Mon-Sat, 1000-1830, Sun 1400-1830, €7 (includes entrance to Treasury, Choir, Sala Capitular, and the Sacristy Museum).* Toledo's vast cathedral, a suitably magnificent home for the Primate See of all Spains, is caught in the bewildering net of narrow streets twisting around its bulk. As a result, it's impossible to see in its entirety, and yet there are tantalizing glimpses of its ancient walls, gates and domes down every tiny passage and square. Begun in 1227 and completed in 1493, it's a complicated mish-mash of Gothic styles, confusing and flouncy on the outside, but exceptionally fine within.

The huge interior, with five broad naves supported by ranks of sturdy columns, is surprisingly light, and the 15th- and 16th-century stained-glass windows are among the finest in Spain. In the middle of the central nave is the elaborate Gothic **Choir**, divided into two tiers of seats. Those on the lower level are intricately carved with scenes from the conquest of Granada, each seat depicting the fall of a different city, and those on the upper levels are etched with biblical stories from the Old Testament and a menagerie of fantastic creatures. The choir is enclosed by a lacy grille originally made of gold, which was given an iron coating to protect it from the pillaging Napoleonic armies; unfortunately, the iron won't come off. The **main altar** is equally flamboyant, with an immense polychrome retablo soaring up to the gilded ceiling, presided over by a 15th-century silver statue of the Virgin. In the ambulatory behind the main altar is an enormous, fluffy **Transparente**, a circular roof opening pierced by theatrical shards of sunlight, surrounded by saints and angels oozing from clouds of plaster. Visit at midday to get the full effect of its kitsch Baroque magnificence, strikingly at odds with the Gothic sobriety of the rest of the church. Below it, a tatty scrap of fabric hangs next to an urn; in fact it's a cardinal's hat, one of several dotted around the cathedral, which mark the burial places of Spanish cardinals who are allowed to choose where they want to be laid to rest. There are dozens of small chapels set into the walls around the cathedral, but the finest is the **Mozarabic chapel** beneath the dome, where Mass is still held according to ancient Visigothic rites daily at 0930 (the only time you'll be able to enter it).

The admission ticket includes entrance to the **Treasury**, with a spectacular *artesonado* ceiling which looks like a melting honeycomb and a 3-m-high 16th-century silver monstrance used in the annual Corpus Christi processions. The **Sacristy** and adjoining rooms contain the cathedral's paintings, notably El Greco's magnificent *El Expolio* (Disrobing of Christ), and works by Rubens, Zurbarán, Titian, Raphael and Caravaggio, as well as a collection of religious ornaments and embroidered vestments dating back to the 15th century. Finally, the **Sala Capitular** contains a blazing scarlet and gold carved ceiling and trompe l'oeil frescoes; in the second hall, there is a series of portraits of the Archbishops of Toledo, the last few all uncannily alike, beneath another gilded ceiling.

On the trail of El Greco The Plaza de Ayuntamiento flanks the eastern side of the cathedral and is overlooked by the 17th-century **Ayuntamiento** (town hall), a restrained, graceful building designed by El Greco's son, Jorge Theotocópuli. Just beyond it is the 16th-century **Convento de Saint Úrsula**, on the little square of the same name, where you can buy some sweet treats from the nuns, and admire the sadly dilapidated Mudéjar carved ceilings (admission €1).

Calle Santo Tomé leads to the **Iglesia Santo Tomé** ① *Plaza del Conde s/n, T925 256 098, www.santotome.org,1000-1800, €2.30*, which contains El Greco's masterful *El Entierro del Conde de Orgaz* (The Burial of Count Orgaz), a massive canvas which established El Greco's reputation once and for all as a spiritual painter par excellence. González Ruiz de Toledo, the fourth Count of Orgaz and tutor to Alfonso XI, was a devout man, and according to legend, Saints Augustine and Stephen miraculously appeared to aid at his burial in this chapel in 1312. The tomb was lost, and remained undiscovered until early 2001. Now the count's bones sit beneath El Greco's solemn, moving depiction of the scene, painted around 1586. The saints, dressed in elaborate robes, are lifting the count into his coffin, while behind them stand a group of influential Toledans in contemporary dress, including, just above St Stephen's head, a self-portrait of El Greco himself. The young boy on the left of the picture is El Greco's beloved son, Jorge, gazing out steadily and inviting the onlooker's participation in the scene. Above the sombre group is a swirl of angels and saints, culminating in the figure of Christ Universal bathed in golden light at the very top. The plain little church contains nothing else of note, besides the tombs of the counts of Fuensalida, whose palace sits opposite the church.

Next door to the Palace of the Counts of Fuensalida is the **Taller de Moro** ① *C/Taller del Moro s/n, T925 227 115, closed for renovation*, a series of rooms in a Mudéjar palace which were used as an atelier for masons working on the cathedral. Much of its original brickwork and decoration have survived, a striking backdrop for a collection of artworks from the period.

Tiny Calle San Juan de Dios, a typical Toledan street lined with an uninterrupted string of souvenir shops, runs down from the church to the **Casa-Museo de El Greco** ① *Paseo del Tránsito s/n, T925 223 665, http://museudelgreco.mcu.es, Apr-Sep Tue-Sat 0930-2000, Sun and hols 1000-1500, Oct-Mar Tue-Sat 0930-1830, Sun 100-1500, €3/€1.50*. It seems unlikely that El Greco ever actually lived here, but it remains a beautiful example of a 16th-century Toledan mansion, with a recreation of El Greco's studio on the upper floor (currently closed for restoration). The adjoining museum displays several of El Greco's masterpieces, including a magnificent *View of Toledo* (1610-1616) in a small chapel with a richly gilded *artesonado* ceiling. There is a gallery of portraits, a series of haunting, melancholy saints, and a room devoted to the works of the Madrid school (which you might happily skip) and another to the Sevilla School, where you'll find a beautiful depiction of the *Tears of St Peter* by Zurbarán (circa 1630-1640).

The Judería This tight spiral of streets around the Casa-Museo de El Greco was once the heart of the Jewish Quarter, or *Judería*. Before the Jews were expelled from Spain in 1492, Toledo had the largest Jewish community on the Iberian peninsula – more than 12,000 Jews lived here, and worshipped at 10 synagogues. Only two survive and both were converted into churches when the Jews were forced into exile. The **Sinagoga del Tránsito** was built in the 13th century with money raised by Samuel Leví, treasurer to Pedro the Cruel (before he lived up to his name and had Samuel executed), and boasts some of the most opulent Mudéjar decoration in all Toledo. There's a magnificent *artesonado* ceiling carved from cedarwood, and the upper walls are adorned with a series of graceful arches and Hebraic inscriptions, thickly encrusted with elaborate mosaics and stucco designs. The annexe, once a convent, has been converted to house the fascinating **Museo Sefardí**

ⓘ *C/Samuel Levi s/n, T925 223 665, Oct-Mar Tue-Sat 0930-1830, Sun 1000-1500, Apr-Sep Tue-Sat 0930-2000, Sun 1000-1500, €3/€1.50*, a museum of Sephardic Jewish culture, with tombs, columns, clothing and books.

The second surviving synagogue is almost next door, just around the corner on Calle Reyes Católicos (ironically named for the monarchs who ordered the expulsion of the Jews). At the end of the 12th century, the **Sinagoga de Santa María la Blanca** ⓘ *1000-1745 (winter) 1000-1900 (summer), €2.50*, was the most important place of worship in Jewish Toledo, but it was also converted into a church on the departure of the Jews. The serene ranks of white horseshoe arches with their pale, intricate decoration have survived intact, and it is still one of the loveliest and most contemplative corners of the city.

At the northeastern end of the Calle Reyes Católicos is the austere **Monasterio de San Juan de los Reyes** ⓘ *Plaza San Juan de los Reyes, T925 223 802, 1000-1730, until 1830 in summer, €2.50*, built in the purest Isabelline Gothic style around a pretty cloister full of orange trees and flowers. The monastery was begun in 1476 by order of the Catholic Kings, Ferdinand and Isabel, to celebrate a victorious battle against the Portuguese and to serve as a Royal Pantheon (until the fall of Granada changed their plans). Their initials are set into the stonework, and the coats of arms of all the kingdoms making up the Spanish Empire at the end of the 15th century are set into the *artesonado* ceiling which surrounds the cloister. The gargoyles and grotesquerie which are massed around the upper gallery of the cloister were a 19th-century addition, but the oddest sight is the great wall covered in chains struck from prisoners released from the Moors after the fall of Granada.

Álcazar (Museo del Ejercito) and around ⓘ *Cuesta de Carlos V, T925 221 673, Tue-Sun 0930-1400, €2*. The Álcazar or fortress sits right on the top of the hill; most of what you see today is a reconstruction, as it was almost entirely demolished during the Civil War. In 1936, almost 1200 Nationalists holed up here for 68 days while the Republican forces bombarded the fortress. This is one of the few places where Franco still gets a good press, with plenty of patriotic plaques, and photos of medal ceremonies for siege-survivors. Most bizarrely, the Nationalist commander's office has been left as it was at the end of the siege to provide a setting for a taped 'genuine' telephone conversation between the commander and his son, who was being held by the Republicans. The Colonel tells his son "Commend your soul to God, shout Viva España, and die like a patriot". The rest of the fortress is an **Army Museum**, with an enormous collection of weaponry, models, medals and uniforms, and you can potter about in the cavernous cellars, where the dormitories and kitchens (which include an oven ingeniously powered by a motorbike) of the besieged families were located.

The transport hub of the old city is the **Plaza Zocodóvar**, which means 'livestock market' and is where the markets, hangings, and bullfights all used to take place. Now it's an elegant, if rather bland, square edged with terrace cafés and cake shops. Almost all the local buses stop here, including those going to and from the train and bus stations.

Almost opposite the square is the **Museo de Santa Cruz** ⓘ *C/Cervantes 3, T925221036, Mon 1000-1830, Tue-Sat 1000-1830, Sun 1000-1430, free*, a former hospital with a dazzling Plateresque façade and a wide, sunny cloister embellished with creamy Mudéjar decoration (a good spot for lazing and reading). The basement contains prehistoric artefacts including the skull and tusks of a couple of mammoths. The painting and sculpture galleries are housed on the ground floor, and include a mixed collection of

16th- and 17th-century religious art, a whole gallery of El Grecos, and the magnificent *Tapis de los Astrolabios* (Signs of the Zodiac), a 15th-century Flemish tapestry. Upstairs is an extensive collection of ceramics from all over Spain.

Puerta de Bisagra and around Calle Armas was once the main road to Madrid, and curves down from Plaza Zocodóvar past a string of churches and medieval gates, before reaching the entrance to the city, the Puerta de Bisagra. On the left, within the city walls, the **Puerta del Sol** is a Mudéjar gateway from the 14th century, and beyond it stands the Mudéjar church of **Santiago El Mayor**. A steep passage leads up to the **Mezquita del Cristo de la Luz**, a 10th-century mosque which was converted into a church in the 13th century, making it possibly the first example of Mudéjar art in Spain. According to legend, Alfonso VI rode into the city on El Cid's horse which suddenly knelt in front of the mosque and refused to take another step. Inside the mosque, a statue of Christ was discovered, illuminated by a lantern which had remained steadily alight for more than three centuries of Moslem rule. The legend gave the church its name – Christ of the Light.

Piercing the city walls is the flamboyant **Puerta Nueva de Bisagra**, still the main entrance to the city from Madrid, which replaced the modest Arabic gateway (still standing next to it) in the mid-16th century, and is topped with the imperial coat of arms of Felipe II. Beyond the gate, outside the city walls and reached through shady gardens with outdoor cafés, is the **Hospital de Tavera** ⓘ *C/Duque de Lerma 2, T925 220 541, Mon-Sat 1000-1430 and 1500-1830, Sun 1000-1430, €4.50, entry by guided tour only,* founded in the 16th century, and restored by the Duchess of Lerma after the Civil War. It's now a quiet and little visited museum, with sumptuous 17th-century apartments hung with paintings by El Greco, Ribera (including the wonderful *Lady with a Beard*), Tintoretto and Zurbarán.

Other churches and museums Toledo is crammed with churches and small museums. **Iglesia de San Román** is one of the oldest churches in Toledo, built with the recycled remnants of Roman columns and Visigothic capitals. It's now the **Museo de los Concilios y de la Cultura Visigótica** ⓘ *Plaza San Román s/n, T925 227 872, Tue-Sat 1000-1400 and 1600-1830, Sun 1000-1400, free,* scattered with Visigothic stonework and jewellery from the fifth and seventh centuries, and still bearing the faded remains of medieval murals on most of the exposed brickwork.

Nearby, on a quiet, dusty square, is the **Convento de Santo Domingo El Antiguo** ⓘ *Plaza Santo Domingo El Antiguo s/n, T925222930, Mon-Sat 1100-1330 and 1600-1900, Sun 1600-1900, €2.* Designed by Herrera in the 16th century, the church is starkly whitewashed which only serves to highlight the beauty of the retablo above the main altar. The panels were painted by El Greco, whose tomb is in the church crypt, and visible through a cracked glass floor. The nuns will let you into the choir to admire their battered collection of religious art – mostly sentimental Baroque bits and bobs – and to pick up some of their famous cakes.

Around Toledo

From Toledo, you can head for the remote hills of the **Montes de Toledo**, pick up pottery from the modern ceramic-producing town of **Talavera de la Reina**, or tilt at windmills like Don Quijote in **Consuegra**.

For Where to stay and Restaurant price codes and other relevant information, see pages 10-19.

San Lorenzo de El Escorial *p75*

El Escorial is an easy day trip from Madrid, but there are a few options for staying if you want to explore the mountains. There are a couple of youth hostels, but they are only open in summer and often full of school groups.

€€€ Hotel Victoria Palace, C/Juan de Toledo 4, T902 570 368, www.nh-hoteles.com. The plushest place in town, with views of the monastery and the surrounding mountains, as well as a pool and expensive, restaurant.

€€ Parrilla Principe, C/Floridablanca 46, T918 901 611, www.parillaprincipe.com. Modest, family-run hotel in a converted 18th-century mansion, with simple but well-equipped rooms and a popular local, mid-range priced restaurant.

€ Camping El Escorial, Ctra de Guadarrama km 14.8, T902 014 900, www.campingel escorial.com. Well-equipped campsite with pools, tennis courts and laundry (nearest bus stop is 500 m).

Sierra de Guadarrama *p76*

For information on the mountain refuges in the Sierra de Guadarrama, consult local tourist offices. In Cercedilla, with so many second homes, there are few accommodation options.

€€-€ Hostal Madrid París, Ctra de Burgos Km 75, Buitrago de Lozoya, T918 681 136. One of only a few options. Simple rooms and a decent restaurant.

€€ El Aribel, Cercedilla, T918 521 511. Simple en suite rooms with pine furniture, an inexpensive restaurant and sunny terrace.

€€ La Barranca, T918 560 368, www.hostallabarranca.com. Simple rooms in a spectacular and secluded mountain setting, with a pool, tennis, terrace bar and mid-range priced restaurant.

€€ Las Postas, Ctra N-601 km 10.20, Navacerrada, T918 560 250, www.hotelas postas.com, is set in a former stage post and has a good bar and mid-range priced restaurant. Comfortable.

€ Youth hostels. There are a couple of hostels further up the village of Cercedilla (**La Dehesas**, T918 520 135, and **Villacastora**, T918 520 334), but they are only open in summer and are almost always booked up by school groups.

Segovia and around *p77, map p78*

€€€ Los Linajes, C/Doctor Velasco 9, T921 460 475, www.hotelloslinjares.com. Occupies part of an 11th-century mansion next to the city walls, but the interior has been over-renovated and rooms are a little sterile.

€€€ Parador de Segovia, Ctra Valladolid s/n, T921 443 737, www.parador.es. Bright, modern and well-equipped parador overlooking a lake, about 2 km outside Segovia, with pool, and fine restaurant. There are fabulous views of Segovia, but you'll need your own transport.

€€ Hostal Don Jaime, C/Ochoa Ondátegui 8, T921 444 787. Right next to the aqueduct and furnished with chintzy fabrics and dark wood.

€€ Hostal Fornos, C/Infanta Isabel 13, T921460198, www.hostalfornos.com. A small, pretty *hostal* just off the Plaza Mayor, with charming rooms decorated with wicker furniture.

€€ Hostería Ayala Berganza, C/Carretas 5, T921 461 300. A charming small hotel in a 15th-century building, with spacious traditional rooms.

€€ Infanta Isabel, Plaza Mayor s/n, T921 461 300, www.hotelinfantaisabel.com. Perfectly placed in a restored 19th-century mansion overlooking the Plaza Mayor, the rooms are large, and the best have balconies on the square.

€€ La Querencia de Valsaín, Carretera de Madrid 39, La Granja de San Ildefonso, T629 652 513, www.laquerenciadevalsain.es. A delightful, eco-friendly rural hotel with a choice of private guest rooms or self-catering accommodation. Ideal base for walking, as well as visiting the royal palace.

€€ Las Sirenas, C/Juan Bravo 30, T921 462 663, www.hotelsirenas.com. A classic hotel built in the 1950s with spacious old-fashioned rooms, a café-bar, and even a gym, in the centre of the old city.

€ Camping Acueducto, Ctra L-601, T921 425 000, www.campingacueducto.com. About 3 km outside town, this is still the closest campsite to Segovia. Take bus No 6 from the centre of town. Open Easter-Sep.

€ Hostal Juan Bravo, C/Juan Bravo 12, T921 463 413. A good, central budget choice, with spotless rooms (with or without bath) and friendly owners.

€ Hostal Plaza, C/Cronista Lecea 11, Segovia, T921 460 303, www.hostal-plaza.com. Simple, friendly guesthouse in a rambling old house just off the Plaza Mayor, with modest rooms at an affordable price.

Ávila *p82, map p84*

€€€€ Palacio de los Velada, Plaza de la Catedral 10, T920 255 100, www.velada hoteles.com. A luxurious 4-star hotel set in a magnificent 16th-century mansion close to the cathedral with a beautiful patio. It does excellent weekend deals – as low as €60 for a double room – if you book early enough.

€€€ Hotel Las Leyendas, C/Francisco Gallego 3, T920 352 042, www.lasleyendas.es. A charming hotel with chic, contemporary rooms in a beautifully renovated 16th-century mansion tucked into the old city walls.

€€€ Parador de Ávila, C/Marqués de Canales y Chozas 2, T920 211 340, www.parador.es. One of the very best paradors, this is housed in a spectacular Renaissance palace and offers lots of luxury

trimmings including antique-decorated rooms and a good restaurant. Prices drop a category in low season.

€€ Las Cancelas, C/Cruz Vieja 6, T920 212 249, www.lascancelas.com. Some of the rustically decorated rooms at this 15th-century inn still contain original fireplaces, and there's an excellent restaurant and tapas bar in the charming patio.

€ Gran Hostal Segundo, C/San Segundo 28, T920 252 590, www.hsansegundo.com. A simple *hostal* in a turn-of-the-century building just outside the city walls; the best rooms have balconies with fantastic views of the cathedral. There's an Italian restaurant and a tapas bar downstairs.

€ Hostal Alcántara, C/Esteban Domingo 11, T920 225 003. Comfortable rooms on a quiet street in the old city.

€ Hostal El Rastro, C/Cepadas s/n (just off Plaza Rastro), T920 352 225. A good budget option in an old mansion within the city walls, with old-fashioned rooms and a good restaurant and tapas bar attached.

Sierra de Gredos *p86*

There is plenty of accommodation in Arenas de San Pedro and plenty of luxury accommodation in Navarredonda.

€€€ Parador de Gredos, Navarredonda, T920 026 200, www.parador.es. A modern parador set in pine forest just outside the village.

€€ La Casa de Arriba, C/de la Cruz, Navarredonda, T920 348 024. A rustic hotel in a sumptuous 17th-century mansion surrounded by gardens.

€€ Casa El Canchal, C/La Fuente 1, Arenas de San Pedro, T920 370 958. A handful of tasteful rooms in a 17th-century mansion. Good value.

€€ El Rinconcito de Gredos, Urb Los Llanos 3-5, Cuevas del Valle, T920 383 288. An attractive mountain hotel, with elegant rooms, beautiful views, and a great restaurant serving sturdy regional cuisine.

€€ La Casa Grande, C/de la Cruz, Navarre-
donda, T920 348 024. A sumptuous 17th-
century mansion surrounded by gardens.
€€ La Casona, Piedrahíta, T920 360 071.
In a 17th-century stone mansion with an
excellent mid-range restaurant.
€ Albergue Juvenil, Navarredonda,
T920 348 005, a well-equipped youth hostel
with a pool and tennis courts; and **El
Almanzor**, Ctra el Barco km 38, Navarredonda,
T920 348 477, which is prettier inside than
you´d expect from the gloomy exterior.
€ Hostal Rural Luna, C/Domingo Labajos 34,
Candelada, T920 382 265, www.lunacande
leda.com. A real charmer, tucked away in
Candelada's historic centre, this lovely little
hotel makes a great base for walkers.
€ La Taberna, C/Carrellana 29, Arenas de
San Pedro, T920 370 395. With a good
cheap café-bar.

Toledo *p91, map p93*
€€€€ Parador Conde de Orgaz,
Cerro del Emperador s/n, T925 221 850,
www.parador.es. 4 km from the centre of the
city, this luxurious parador has fantastic views
of Toledo from the pool and terrace, old
beamed ceilings and antique-filled rooms.
The restaurant serves good Toledan
specialities including stewed partridge.
€€€ Alfonso VI, C/General Moscardó 2,
T925 222 600. A plush option inside the city
walls, this is a vigorously converted mansion
near Plaza Zocodovar, with all the trimmings
including a restaurant and tapas bar.
€€ Hostal del Cardenal, Paseo de Recaredo
24, T925 224 900, www.hostaldelcardenal.es.
Formerly the home of Cardinal Lorenzana of
the Inquisition, this magnificent stone palace
is set in shady gardens in the heart of old
Toledo. The rooms are traditionally decorated
with carved wooden beds and old prints, and
the restaurant (**La Antigua Casa del Sobrino
de Botín** or 'the old restaurant of Botín's
nephew', Botín being the name of Madrid's
oldest tavern) is one of the best in the city.

€€ La Almunia de San Miguel, C/San
Miguel 12, T925 257 772, www.almuniade
sanmiguel.com. An immaculately restored
17th-century townhouse close to the Alcázar,
complete with wooden beams and interior
patio. There's a terrace in the attic with
stunning views.
€€ Hostal Centro, C/Nueva 13,
T925 257 091. Probably the best budget
option in Toledo, this offers sparkling new
rooms with a/c in a great location just off the
Plaza Zocodovar.
€€ Hostal La Posada de Manolo,
C/Sixto Ramón Parro 8, T955 282 250,
www.laposadademanolo.com. A simple
yet charming guesthouse with
rustically decorated rooms and a
warm welcome.
€€ Hotel Santa Isabel, C/Santa Isabel 24,
T925 253 120. A central, much-modernized
townhouse down a quiet street close to the
cathedral, with large rooms and tiled patios.
The rooms in the new annexe, another
modernized old mansion with beams,
are the best.
€ Albergue Juvenil, Castillo San Servando,
T925 224 558. Set in a wing of a 14th-century
castle with beautiful views of the city, this
youth hostel fills up quickly. Note that it
closes from mid-Aug until mid-Sep.
€ Camping El Greco, Ctra Toledo–
Puebla Montalbán km 0.7, T925 220 090,
www.campingelgreco.es. The best of the
3 campsites near Toledo, this is a good
30-min walk away from the town centre,
but has a pool, laundry, pizzeria and good
views of the city.
€ Hostal Madrid, C/Marqués de Mendigorria
7, T925 221 114. Simple, central and popular,
this good-value *hostal* has great views from
some rooms.
€ Pensión Castilla, C/Recoletos 6,
T925 256 318. Tucked down a tiny passage,
this old-fashioned friendly *pensión* with
tiled entrance offers basic rooms at a
basic price.

El Escorial *p75*

€€ **Charolés**, C/Floridablanca 24, T918 905 975. This is El Escorial's most celebrated restaurant; the Wed *cocido* is an institution. Terrace in summer.

€€ **Fonda Genara**, Plaza San Lorenzo, T918 903 033. Tucked between 2 squares, this traditional, elegant restaurant serves home-cooked dishes.

€ **La Cueva**, C/San Antón 4, T918 901 516. Another popular spot, **La Cueva** is a delightfully rickety old inn set over 3 floors which offers tapas in the bar or tasty, cheap, local dishes in the dining area.

Sierra de Guadarrama *p76*

In Buitrago de Lozoya, the Plaza de la Constitución, just outside the old walls, is lined with restaurants and bars, most of which have terraces out on the square in summer. See Where to stay for other options.

Segovia and around *p77, map p78*

Segovia's legendary speciality is *cochinillo asado* (roast suckling pig), traditionally slaughtered at just 21 days old. The expensive restaurants at the **Hosteria Ayala Berganza** and the **parador** (see page 98) are also recommended.

€€€ **Méson de Cándido**, Plaza Azoguejo 5, T921 425 911, www.mesondecandido.es. The late Señor Cándido was a legend, and his restaurant, picturesquely huddled under the aqueduct arches, is papered with photos of famous clients. Now run by his son, its reputation has palled slightly, but it's still a memorable spot.

€€€ **Mesón de José María**, C/Cronista Lecea 11, T921 461 111. Cándido's former pupil José María has been making a very big name for himself at his own *méson*, which is rated as one of the very best restaurants in Segovia and is a great place to try *cochinillo*. There's a lively bar area for tapas if you don't want a big meal.

€€ **Casa Duque**, C/Cervantes 12, T921 462 487. Another local institution, with an excellent reputation for traditional Segovian cuisine. It's generally considered to make the best *cochinillo asado* in Segovia, and the *judiones* (another local dish of beans cooked with pork) are also very tasty.

€€ **Dólar**, C/Valenciana 1, T921 470 269. Traditional Castillian cuisine in an elegant dining room in San Ildefonso de la Granja.

€€ **El Bernadino**, C/Cervantes 2, T921 462 477. A classic Castillian restaurant which is popular with local business people, and does an excellent *menú del día*. Try the amazing *sopa de chocolate* for dessert.

€€ **Riofrío**, T921 480 061. The restaurant at the palace is surprisingly good, open lunchtimes only when you can tuck into *sopa castellana* or roast suckling pig.

€ **Cueva de San Estabán**, C/Valdeláguila 15, Segovia, T921 460 982. This cavernous bar-restaurant just off the Plaza San Estabán is a big favourite with locals. Good tapas and a reasonably priced *menú del día* – going a la carte will up the prices considerably.

€ **Mesón Mayor**, Plaza Mayor 3, T921 463 017, www.mesonmayor.com. The best of the restaurants on the Plaza Mayor, you can tuck into roast meats or fill up on good tapas.

Tapas bars and cafés

In San Ildefonso de la Granja there are many tapas bars clustered on the Plaza de los Dolores. The following are all in Segovia.

El Sitio, C/Infanta Isabel 9. Classic tapas and plenty of atmosphere at this old-fashioned local favourite.

La Barcaza, C/Gobernador Fernández Jiménez 22. A quiet spot for some tasty tapas including fish with wild mushrooms, and local *morcilla* (blood sausage).

Limón y Menta, C/Infanta Isabel 3, T921 462 141. A friendly little café and cake shop serving good *bocadillos* and pastries that won't break the bank.

Ávila *p82, map p84*

The restaurants at the **parador**, the **Hostería de Bracamonte**, **Las Cancelas** (all €€€-€€) and the **Mesón del Rastro** (€€-€) are all recommended (see above). They all serve an excellent value *menú del día* at lunchtimes – often for less than €15.

€€ Alcaravea, Plaza de la Catedral 15, T920 226 600. A sumptuous old mansion, serving refined regional cuisine. Great summer terrace.

€€ Fogón de Santa Teresa, Plaza de la Catedral, T920 211 023. Sturdy Castillian favourites made with the freshest local produce. This is a good place to try *perdiz* (partridge), a local speciality and apparently one of Saint Teresa's favourites.

€€ La Casona, Plaza Pedro Dávila, T920 256 139. Small, family-run local, serving big portions of good home-cooking in a prettily tiled dining room.

€ Casa Patas, C/San Millán 4, T920 213 194. A local stalwart, this old-fashioned bar serves good tapas and simple meals.

Tapas bars and cafés

Bodeguita de San Segundo, C/San Segundo 19, T920 257 309. A smart tapas and wine bar which attracts a well-heeled crowd and gets packed out in the evenings.

Aranjuez *p89*

€€€ Casa José, C/Abastos 32, T918 911 418. Sublime contemporary cuisine and a beautiful dining room combine to make for an unforgettable experience.

€€ La Rana Verde, C/Reina 1, T918 913 238, you'll get reasonable, if unexceptional, food but a lovely riverside setting. The local specialities are strawberries and asparagus – if you arrive on the strawberry train, they'll serve you local strawberries on the way.

Chinchón *p90*

Good traditional *mesónes* on the Plaza Mayor include **€€ Mesón de la Virreina**, T918 940 015, and **€€ La Balconada**, T918 941 303.

€€ Mesón Cuevas del Vino, C/Benito Hortelano 13, T918 940 206. Set in a former olive oil mill and has a particularly good, mid-range priced wine list.

€ El Comendador, Plaza Mayor 21, T918 940 420. Good-value set meals make this a stand-out option in Chinchón's main square.

Toledo *p91, map p93*

€€€ Asador Adolfo, C/Hombre de Palo 7, T925 337 321. This is the most celebrated restaurant in town, with a sumptuous dining room serving excellent regional dishes, particularly good roast meats, accompanied by an equally fine wine list.

€€€ Casón de los López de Toledo, C/Sillería 3, T925 254 774. A charming, beautifully renovated old mansion, serving sturdy *manchega* dishes and regional wines.

€€ La Abadía, C/Nuñez de Arce 3, T925 251 140. This restaurant and bar is enormously popular with locals who spill out on the street with their drinks. Excellent tapas and a good value *menú del día*.

€€ La Perdiz, C/Reyes Católicos 7, T925 252 919. The speciality here is, of course, pheasant, served in a dozen different ways.

€ Casa Ludeña, Plaza de la Magdalena 13, T925 223 384. A very friendly, old-fashioned restaurant serving Toledano classics like partridge or *cuchifrito* (lamb cooked in sauce of tomatoes, egg, wine and saffron). Good value *menú del día*.

€ La Virgen de la Estrella, C/Alrosas 1, T925 253 134. Small old-fashioned and family-run, this serves home-cooking and a great-value *menú del día* €10. Ideal for trying Toledano classics.

€ Mille Grazie, C/Cadenas 2, T925 254 270. This is the best of Toledo's Italian restaurants, with tasty pizzas (including some veggie options), Italian cured hams – and long queues at weekends. Set lunch for €12.

Tapas bar and cafés

Albaicín, Plaza de Cuba s/n. Tiny bar in the new part of town, serving tasty *pintxos* – chunks of baguette with all kinds of toppings.

Cervecería Adolfo, C/Nuncio Viejo, 1. Attached to the celebrated restaurant, this offers high-quality tapas at a price to match.

El Trébol, C/Santa Fe 5. Buzzy lively little bar, which also does a fantastic range of tapas and raciones, including the house specialities – *bombas*, fried balls of mashed potato with a spicy sauce.

La Cepa Andaluza, C/Méjico, 11. A small, local bar serving fantastic *frituras de pescado*, tasty fried fish in the Andaluz style.

La Flor de la Esquina, Plaza Juan de Mariana 2, www.laflordelaesquina.com. A revamped old taverna serving delicious tapas – both traditional and modern recipes. Also good for breakfasts, sandwiches and drinks.

🜨 Bars and clubs

Segovia and around *p77, map p78*

C/Infanta Isabel has got so many bars that it's known locally as 'Calle de los Bares'. There are dozens to choose from, such as the popular **Geografic Chic**, at No 13, which is decorated with comic-book characters. **Compás**, at C/Santo Tomás 1, and **Cuba Libre** at C/Ochoa Andoátegui 8 are both good for cocktails, and **Bar Santana**, C/ de la Infanta Isabel 18, T921 463 564, www.barsantana.com, has live gigs, art exhibitions, tapas and more on offer.

Ávila *p82, map p84*

Ávila isn't a great city for nightlife, but there are plenty of bars and cafés around the Plaza de la Victoria, and the Plaza de Santa Teresa and the streets which lead off them.

Toledo *p91, map p93*

Toledo's nightlife is pretty low-key for a student city of its size, and the *tapeo* is more of an institution than serious drinking or clubbing sessions – except in summer when everyone piles down to the big outdoor discos by the river, or along the Paseo del Miradero at the northern end of town. There are bars and clubs to suit most tastes in Toledo's *casco histórico*, and there are plenty more in the streets around the Plaza Cuba in the new part of town – **Albaicín** and **Trebol** (see above) are both good for a chilled beer on a hot night. For alternative, studenty bars, try the Callejón Sillería and around for jazz and blues, or head for **El Último** on Plaza Colegio Infantes 4, T925212236, which has occasional live music. **Picaro**, C/Cadenas, has concerts and DJ sessions, see www.picarao.com for the programme.

✱ Festivals

Segovia and around *p77, map p78*
There's usually something going on in Segovia.
Nearest Sun to 5 Feb Fiesta de Santa Águeda when Segovian women take over the city for a day to celebrate this festival.
Holy Week A big event with plenty of processions.
24-29 Jun Fiestas of San Juan and San Pedro are celebrated with street parties and parades.
Jul A classical music festival.

Ávila *p82, map p84*
Unsurprisingly, Ávila's festivals are more serious than most.
Oct Santa Teresa is remembered with *verbenas* and religious ceremonies, floods of pilgrims descend on the city.
Easter week Parades, processions and Mass.
Jul A festival of **organ music**.

Toledo *p91, map p93*
Late May or early Jun Corpus Christi is Toledo's most important festival with a spectacular, solemn procession through the streets. **Holy Week** is also an important event.

☉ Shopping

Toledo *p91, map p93*
Toledo has long been famous for its steel, and particularly for its knives. The city has dozens of gift shops selling armour, swords, etc: particularly in Calles Commercio and Ancha around the cathedral. If you like kitsch, these shops are definitely worth a rummage for quirky souvenirs.

You'll find ceramics and Jewish-related souvenirs in the Calle Santo Tomé and around, and you can pick up some of the city's famous *mazapan* sweets in the convents, or, more mundanely, in one of the delicious cake shops on the Plaza Zocodovar; *Santo Tomé*, at No 11, is regarded as the finest.

⚠ What to do

Sierra de Guadarrama *p76*
There are 2 small low-key ski resorts less than 70 km from Madrid: neither is particularly high, and the slopes are short and not very demanding, but at least you can easily get there just for the day. *Tren de la Nieve* ('Snow Train') runs between Cercedilla and the slopes of Navacerrada and Cotos-Valdesquí.
Puerto de Navacerrada, 60 km north of Madrid, T902 882 328, www.puertodenavacerrada.com, with 14 slopes, 5 chair lifts, 3 ski lifts. Shuttle buses leave regularly from Navacerrada for the ski station.
Valdesquí, 73 km north of Madrid, www.valdesqui.com, with 26 slopes, 6 chairlifts, 6 ski lifts and 2 children's ski lifts.

Sierra de Gredos *p86*
AMN (**AMN Gredos**), T920 348 385, www.amngredos.com. Offers all kinds of activities from rafting to hang-gliding.
Gredos a Caballo, T920 348 110, www.gredasacaballo.com, organizes horse-riding expeditions from Hoyos del Espino.

⊖ Transport

El Escorial and the Sierra de Guadarrama *p75*
Bus and train San Lorenzo de Escorial is reached by regular buses (**Herranz**, T918 969 028) and trains (from Atocha) from Madrid. One bus daily leaves from El Escorial for **Valle de los Caídos** at 1515, returns at 1730. **Cercedilla** and **Cotos** (for the **Parque Natural de Peñalara** and the ski station at **Puerto Navacerrada**) are also on the regional train line (C2 and C8B from Chamartín station in Madrid). Bus 724 leaves from the Plaza Castilla in **Madrid** for **Manzanares el Real**. There are daily direct buses to **Buitrago de Lozoya** from Madrid's Estación de Sur bus station (route No 191).

Segovia and around *p77, map p78*
Bus Bus is the most convenient way to reach Segovia. There are regular services (every 30 mins) with **La Sepulvedana**, T902 1196, www.lasepulvadena.es, from Paseo de la Florida 11, Madrid (Metro Principe Pío); 1½ hrs journey time, €7.66. There are local (6 times daily) buses from Segovia to **La Granja**, but you'll need your own transport to get out to **Riofrío**, which is about 10 km south of Segovia.
Train Trains depart every 2 hrs from Atocha; 1 hr 45 mins journey time, €7 one way.

Ávila *p82, map p84*
Bus Buses leave every 2 hrs from the Estación Sur in Madrid with **Larrear** (T915 304 800); 1¾ hrs, €7. Trains take 1½ hrs and cost €6.50. There are about 4 buses daily to **Salamanca**;1½ hrs, €5 and up to 7 buses daily for **Segovia** (1 hr, €4).
Train Train services are frequent to **Chamartín** and **Atocha** in Madrid, as well as connections to Salamanca, Valladolid, Medina del Campo and El Escorial.

Sierra de Gredos p86
Bus Buses from Madrid (4 times daily), from Escación and Ávila (1 daily) to **Arenas de San Pedro**, with once-daily connections to Guisando, El Arenal and El Hornillo on weekdays. There are 3 buses daily with **Cevesa**, T902 393 132, www.cevesa.es, from Ávila to **Piedrahíta** and **El Barco** and 4 buses daily from Madrid.

Aranjuez p89
Bus There are regular buses to Aranjuez from **Madrid**'s Estación Sur (**AISA**, T902 198 788); 1 hr.

Train Trains run every 10 mins on the Guadalajara line from Atocha; 45 mins. In summer, the *Tren de la Fresa* ('Strawberry Train') steams to **Aranjuez** from Atocha station on summer weekends from late Apr until mid-Oct. For more information visit www.aranjuez.net.

Toledo p91, map p93
Bus Bus services with **ALSA**, T902 422 242, www.alsa.es, to **Madrid** every 30 mins, with an express service every hour. Various companies run services to **Ciudad Real**, Cuenca, **Albacete**, **Alcázar de San Juan** and there are local buses to **Orgaz**, **La Puebla de Montalbán**, and **Talavera de la Reina** (which has onward connections to **Extremadura**). For bus information, call Toledo bus station, T925 215 850.

Train Trains run frequently to **Aranjuez** (up to 9 daily, 45 mins) and **Madrid** (9 daily, 1¾ hrs). Toledo and Madrid are connected by an express train service.

❸ Directory

Segovia and around p77, map p78
Banks There are plenty around the Plaza Mayor. In Piedrahíta, there are plenty of banks and ATMs, especially around the Plaza de Santa Teresa. **Post office** Plaza de los Huertos 5. The main post office in Piedrahíta is on the Plaza Catédral 2.

Toledo p91, map p93
Banks You'll find plenty of banks throughout the city, but there are dozens of ATMs on and around the Plaza Zocodovar. All the banks have bureaux de change. **Post office** The main post office is in the centre of the old city on Calle de la Plata 1.

Contents

108 Architecture

115 Art

Background

Architecture

Spain's architectural heritage is one of Europe's richest and certainly its most diverse, due in a large part to the dual influences of European Christian and Islamic styles during the eight centuries of Moorish presence in the peninsula. Another factor is economic; both during the Reconquista and in the wake of the discovery of the Americas, money seemed limitless, and vast building projects were undertaken. The post-Reconquista decline of Northern Spain, coupled with the bankruptcy of Imperial Spain, although not an ideal situation at the time, has at least had a good effect. The building sprees of the Middle Ages in Spain's north were succeeded by periods where there was hardly any money to fund new construction; the result is a land which has an incredibly rich architectural heritage. Nowhere in Europe has such a wealth of Romanesque and Gothic churches. In the south, entire treasure fleets were spent in erecting lavish churches and monasteries on previously Muslim soil, while relationships with Islamic civilization spawned some fascinating styles unique to Spain. The Moors themselves adorned their towns with incredibly sensuous palaces, such as Granada's Alhambra, and elegant mosques, as well as employing compact urban planning that still forms the hearts of most Andalucían towns. In modern times Spain has shaken off the ponderous monumentalism of the Franco era and become something of a powerhouse of modern architecture, with the Basque lands jostling Valencia at the front of the pack.

Prehistoric structures

There are some very early stone structures in the peninsula, with the greatest concentration in Álava and in Galicia, and the finest examples from around Antequera, in Andalucía. Dolmens, menhirs and standing stone circles are the most common remnants of the Neolithic (late Stone Age) era. The first two mostly had a funerary function, while the latter are the subject of numerous theories; some sort of religious/astrological purpose seems likely, but an accurate explanation is unlikely to emerge. The dwellings of the period were less permanent structures of which little evidence remains.

Celts and Iberians

The first millennium BC saw the construction of sturdier settlements, usually on hilltops. The sizeable Iberian town of Numancia, though razed after a Roman siege, remains an interesting example, and many of the cities of Northern Spain were originally founded during this period. The Celts, too, favoured hilly locations for the construction of castros. These fort/villages were typically walled compounds containing a large building, presumably the residence of the chieftain and hall for administration and trading, surrounded by smaller, circular houses and narrow lanes. These dwellings were probably built from mudbrick/adobe on a stone foundation with a thatched roof. The Galician palloza, still seen in villages, has probably changed little since these times. There are many preserved castros in Northern Spain, principally in Galicia and western Asturias.

Phoenicians, Greeks and Carthaginians

While the Phoenicians established many towns in Southern Spain, and probably a few on the north coast, their remains are few; the Phoenicians were so adept at spotting natural harbours that nearly all have been in continual use ever since, leaving only the odd foundations or breakwaters.

Greek trading presence has left a similarly scant architectural legacy but one site, Empúries, stands out. An important Mediterranean trading post (the name means 'market'), there are remains of a forum, a defensive wall, a harbour and a temple to Asklepeius, a standard arrangement for such a place.

There are also few Carthaginian remains of note. Their principal capital was Cádiz, but two millennia of subsequent occupation have taken their toll, and Cartagena, named for Carthage, preserves similarly scant remnants.

Roman period

The story of Spanish architecture really began with the Romans, who colonized the peninsula and imposed their culture on it to a significant degree. The Roman occupation of Hispania was largely administered from the south and east, and the majority of architectural remains are in that region. They founded and took over a great number of towns; most of the provincial capitals of Spain sit on Roman foundations. More significant still is the legacy they left; architectural principles that endured and to some extenet formed the basis for later peninsular styles.

There's not a wealth of outstanding monuments, the theatre and town of Mérida is the finest, while the Segovia aqueduct, the (modified) fantastic walls of Lugo and the bridge at Alcántara are imposing single structures. Itálica, Clunia and Numancia are impressive, if not especially well-preserved, Roman towns, as are Sagunto and Bilbilis. Tarragona and Zaragoza also were important towns, and preserve some decent ruins, while some fine villas are to be found in the south and also in Palencia province. While not exactly architecture, the awesome landscape of the mines of Las Médulas in western León province attest to the engineering prowess and single-mindedness of the Roman occupancy.

Visigothic Period

Although the post-Roman period is often characterized as a time of lawless barbarism, the Visigoths added Germanic elements to Roman and local traditions and built widely; in particular the kings of the period commissioned many churches. Most of these were heavily modified or destroyed in succeeding periods, but a few excellent examples remain; the best are San Juan de Baños (near Palencia), Quintanilla de las Viñas (near Burgos), San Pedro de la Nave (near Zamora). All these date from the seventh century and are broadly similar. Sturdy yet not unelegant, these churches are built around a triple nave with short transepts and square apses. Friezes on the outside depict birds, fruit and flowers with some skill. The interiors are particularly attractive, with treble arches, frequently horseshoe-shaped, and altarstones. These altarstones are found in many other churches of later date and are interesting for their iconography; early Christian symbols heavily borrowed from pagan traditions. Depictions of the sun, moon, and crops are often accompanied by Celtic-like circles with arched spokes. Mérida then Toledo were Visigothic capitals but preserve few remains of the period.

Moorish period

The first distinct period of Moorish architecture in Spain is that of the Umayyads ruling as emirs, then as caliphs, from Córdoba from the eighth to 11th centuries. The massive arched Mezquita is the standout building from this period. Added to by different rulers, it's an amazing mosque flanked by the characteristic courtyard for ablutions. The exterior features several fine doorways, and the interior use of alternating red brick and white stone was an innovation. Other impressive buildings from this period and the taifa period that followed it include the palace complex at nearby Medina Azahara, the Aljafería palace at Zaragoza (although much modified subsequently) and the mosque of Cristo de la Luz in Toledo. Many defensive installations were also put up at this time; the proud castle of Gormaz in Soria province, and several of the Alcazabas of Andalucían towns: Almería and Málaga being especially impressive. Architectural features of the period included use of the horseshoe arch, the multifoil arch, ornate raised brickwork, and inner courtyards. Highly elaborate plaster and tiled decoration was favoured:

Once the caliphate disintegrated, the Almohads brought their own architectural modifications with them. Based in Sevilla, their styles were not as flamboyant, and relied heavily on ornamental brickwork. The supreme example of the period is the Giralda tower that once belonged to the Mosque in Sevilla – it now forms part of the cathedral. The use of intricate wood-panelled ceilings began to be popular, and the characteristic Andalucían azulejo decorative tiles were first used at this time. Over this period the horseshoe arch developed a point.

The climax of Moorish architecture ironically came when Al-Andalus was already doomed and had been reduced to the emirate of Granada. Under the Nasrid rulers of that city the sublime Alhambra was constructed; a palace and pleasure-garden that took elegance and sophistication in architecture to previously unseen levels. Nearly all the attention was focused on the interior of the buildings, which consisted of galleries and courtyards offset by water features and elegant gardens. The architectural high point of this and other buildings is the sheer intricacy of the stucco decoration in panels surrounding the windows and doorways. Another ennobling feature is mocárabes, a curious concave decoration of prisms placed in a cupola or ceiling and resembling natural crystal formations in caves. The alcázar in Sevilla is also a good example of the period, albeit constructed in Christian Spain.

Christian architecture

In the eighth century, the style known as Pre-Romanesque emerged in the Christian redoubt of Asturias. While there are clear similarities to the Visigothic style, the Asturians added some elements and created a series of buildings of striking beauty, many of which are well-preserved today. The style progressed considerably in a fairly short period. There are both churches and royal halls extant. The buildings are generally tripartite, with triple naves (or nave and two aisles) and arches (some exterior) resting on elegantly carved pillars. The small windows reflect this in miniature, often divided by a bonsai column. The floor plan is rectangular or that of a cross, with wide transepts; the altar area is often raised, and backed by three small apses, divided from the rest of the interior by a triple arch. Small domes were used in later examples. Narrow exterior buttresses line up with the interior arches. Mural painting is well-preserved in many of the buildings; the Asturian (Latin) cross is a frequent motif. The capitals of the pillars are in some cases finely carved, in many cases with motifs presumably influenced by contact with Moorish and Byzantine civilization; palm leaves, flowers, and curious beasts.

During the Muslim occupation of Northern Spain a distinctly Moorish style was used by Christian masons, particularly in church construction. These traditions persisted even after reconquest, and were strengthened by the arrival of Christians who had lived in the

Muslim south. Known as Mozarabic, it is characterized above all by its horseshoe arches but in some cases also by exuberant fan vaulting and ornate ribbed ceilings; some of the churches feel far more Muslim than Christian. The style persisted, and even some of the most sober of later cathedrals and churches have the odd arch or two that bends a little further in. Fresco-work is present in some Mozarabic buildings too, and in some cases, such as the Ermita de San Baudelio (Berlanga de Duero) presents a fusion of scenes; some from orthodox Christian iconography, and some influenced by time spent in Moorish company; elephants, camels, and palm trees.

Romanesque

The style that spread across the whole of Northern Spain in the 11th and 12th centuries, and is most dear to many visitors' hearts, is the Romanesque or románico. The 'Catalan' style, derived from contact with Italy, features the Lombard arch (blind exterior decoration in the shape of fingers) as a primary characteristic. In the rest of northern Spain, Romanesque can be traced back to French influences. Many monks from France arrived in the north of the peninsula in the 11th century and built monasteries along the same lines as the ones of their home country, but the biggest single factor in the spread of the style was the Santiago pilgrimage. News of what was being built in the rest of Europe was spread across Northern Spain and it is fitting that the portal of the cathedral at Santiago is widely considered to be the pinnacle of Spanish Romanesque.

The typical features of Romanesque churches are barrel-vaulted ceilings (stone roofs considerably reduced the number of churches that burned down) with semi circular arches; these also appear on the door and window openings. The apse(s) is also round. Geometric decoration is common, such as the chessboard patterning known as ajedrezado jaqués, first known in the Pyrenean town of Jaca, from where it spread along the length of the pilgrim route. Fine carvings, once painted, are often present on capitals and portals; the cloisters of Santo Domingo de Silos and San Juan de la Peña as well as the church San Martín in Frómista are excellent examples. The carvings depict a huge variety of subjects; Biblical scenes are present, and vegetable motifs recurring, but scenes of everyday life from the sublime to the ridiculous, the mundane to the erotic, are common (and often dryly labelled 'allegorical' in church pamphlets), as are strange beasts and scenes from mythology. This is part of the style's charm, as is the beautifully homely appearance of the buildings, often built from golden stone. Some of the towns with an excellent assembly of the Romanesque are Soria and Zamora, as well as all along the Camino de Santiago and in Catalunya, but the purest examples are often in the middle of nowhere; places where someone had the money to build a stone church in the 11th century, and no-one's had the cash to meddle with it since.

Transitional architecture

Austerity in monastic life ushered in the change from Romanesque to Gothic; a preference for elegant remote purity. The whimsical carved capitals disappeared, and voluptuous curves were squared off as church authorities began to exert more control within their dioceses. Cathedral such as those of Zamora, Salamanca (the old one), Tarragona, Ávila and Sigüenza are all good examples; in many cases the religious buildings were heavily fortified.

Gothic

It seems unbelievable that the word Gothic was originally a pejorative term, applied to the pointed style during the Baroque period to mean 'barbarous'. Spanish Gothic architecture also owed much to French influence, although German masons and master builders also did much work, particularly in and around Burgos. Advances in engineering allowed lighter, higher structures than their Romanesque forebears, and the wealth and optimism of the rapidly progressing Reconquista saw ever more imaginative structures raised. The cathedrals of León and Burgos are beautiful examples of this. Other examples of Spanish Gothic are the cathedrals of Girona, Toledo and Sevilla, among many.

Gothic architecture changed over time from its relatively restrained 13th century beginnings to a more extroverted style known as Flamboyant, but many of the basic features remained constant. The basic unit of Gothic is the pointed arch, symbolic of the general enthusiasm for 'more space, less stone' that pervaded the whole endeavour. The same desire was behind the flying buttress, an elegant means of supporting the building from the exterior, thus reducing the amount of interior masonry. Large windows increased the amount of light; the rose window is a characteristic feature of many Gothic façades, while the amount of stained glass in León seems to defy physics (to the regular concern of engineers). Elaborate vaulting graced the ceilings. The groundplan was often borrowed from French churches; as the style progressed, more and more side chapels were added, particularly around the ambulatory. A feature of many Spanish Gothic churches is the enclosed coro (choir, or chancel) in the middle of the nave, a seemingly self-defeating placement that robs the building of much of the sense of space and light otherwise striven for. Nevertheless, the choirstalls are often one of the finest features of Gothic architecture, superbly carved in wood.

Ornate carved decoration is common on the exteriors of Gothic buildings. Narrow pinnacles sprout like stone shoots, and the façades are often topped by gables. Portals often feature piers and tympanums carved with Biblican figures and scenes, circled by elaborate archivolts.

The late 15th century saw a branching-off: the Isabelline style, which borrowed decorative motifs from Islamic architecture to adorn a basically Gothic structure.

Mudéjar

As the Reconquista took town after town from the Muslims, Moorish architects and those who worked with them began to meld their Islamic tradition with the northern influences of Romanesque and Gothic. The result is distinctive and pleasing, typified by the decorative use of brick and coloured tiles, with the tall elegant belltowers a particular highlight. Another common feature is the highly elaborate wooden panelled ceilings, some of which are masterpieces. The word *artesonado* describes the most characteristic type of these. The style became popular nationwide; in certain areas, Mudéjar remained a constant feature for over 500 years of building. Aragón, which had a strong Moorish population, has a particularly fine collection of Mudéjar architecture; Toledo, Sevilla, the Duero valley and Sahagún are also well-stocked.

Renaissance

The 16th century was a high point in Spanish power and wealth, when it expanded across the Atlantic, tapping riches that must have seemed limitless for a while. Spanish

Renaissance architecture reflected this, leading from the late Gothic style into the elaborate peninsular style known as Plateresque. Although the style originally relied heavily on Italian models, it soon took on specifically Spanish features. The word refers particularly to the façades of civil and religious buildings, characterized by decoration of shields and other heraldic motifs, as well as geometric and naturalistic patterns such as shells. The term comes from the word for silversmith, platero, as the level of intricacy of the stonework approached that of jewellery. Arches went back to the rounded, and columns and piers became a riot of foliage and 'grotesque' scenes. The massive façade of San Marcos in León is an excellent example of the style, as is the university at Salamanca, and several buildings in Toledo.

A classical revival put an end to much of the elaboration, as Renaissance architects concentrated on purity. Classical Greek features such as fluted columns and pediments were added to by large Italianate cupolas and domes. Spanish architects were apprenticed to Italian masters and returned with their ideas. Elegant interior patios in palacios are an especially attractive feature of the style, to be found across the country. Andalucía is a particularly rich storehouse of this style, where the master Diego de Siloé designed numerous cathedrals and churches. The palace of Carlos V in the Alhambra grounds is often cited as one of the finest examples, and the north has plenty too, particularly in Salamanca, as well as Valladolid and smaller places such as Medina del Campo. The Escorial, the severe palace built for Philip II, is perhaps the ultimate expression of Spanish Renaissance architecture: grand yet austere, on a massive scale, it represents all the power and introversion of Imperial Spain.

Baroque
The fairly pure lines of this Renaissance classicism were soon to be permed into a new style; Spanish Baroque. Although it started fairly soberly, it soon became quite an ornamental style, often being used to add elements to existing buildings, with greater or lesser success. Nevertheless, the Baroque was a time of great genius in architecture as in the other arts in Spain. Perhaps the finest Baroque structures in Spain are to be found in Galicia, where masons had to contend with granite and hence dedicated themselves to overall appearances rather than obsessive and intricate twirls. The façade of the cathedral at Santiago, with its soaring lines, is one of the best of many examples. Compared to granite, sandstone can be carved as easily as Play-Doh, and architects in the rest of Spain playfully explored the reaches of their imaginations; a strong reaction against the sober preceding style. Churches became ever larger – in part to justify the huge façades – and nobles indulged in one-upmanship, building ever-grander palacios. The façades themselves are typified by such features as pilasters (narrow piers descending to a point) and niches to hold statues. On a private residence, large sculptured coats-of-arms were de rigueur. The cathedral at Cádiz is one of the few wholly Baroque churches.

Churrigueresque
The most extreme form of Spanish Baroque, Churrigueresque, which has been not too harshly described as 'architectural decay', was named for the Churriguera brothers who took Spanish Baroque to an extreme of ornamentation in the late 17th and early 18th centuries. The result can be hideously overelaborate but on occasion transcendentally beautiful, like Salamanca's superb Plaza Mayor. Vine tendrils decorate the façades, which

seem intent on breaking every classical norm, twisting here, upside-down there but often straying into the realm of the conceited.

Neo-classicism

Neo-classicism was an inevitable reaction to such frippery, encouraged by a new interest in the ancient civilizations of Greece and Rome. It again resorted to the cleaner lines of antiquity, which were used this time for public spaces as well as civic and religious buildings. Many plazas and town halls in Spain are in this style, which tended to flourish in the cities that were thriving in the late 18th and 19th centuries, such as Madrid, Bilbao and A Coruña. The best examples use symmetry to achieve beauty and elegance, such as the Prado in Madrid, the worst achieve only narrow-minded lifelessness.

Modernista

The late 19th century saw Catalan modernista architecture break the moulds in a startling way. At the forefront of the movement was Antoni Gaudí. Essentially a highly original interpretation of Art Nouveau, Gaudí's designs featured naturalistic curves and contours enlivened with stylistic elements inspired by Muslim and Gothic architecture. Most of the most startling modernista works are in his home city of Barcelona, but there are examples throughout Spain, notably in Comillas on the Cantabrian coast. Gaudí's master work, the Sagrada Familia, is steadily being completed: although he spent half his life on the building, it was never going to be enough for such a deeply imaginative design. More restrained fin de siècle architecture can be seen in the fashionable towns of San Sebastián, Madrid, Santander, and A Coruña, as well as the industrial powerhouses of Gijón, Almería and Bilbao.

Art Nouveau and Art Deco

At roughly the same time, and equally a break with the academicism of the last century, Art Nouveau aimed to bring art back to life and back to the everyday. Using a variety of naturalistic motifs to create whimsical façades and objets, the best Art Nouveau works manage to combine elegance with fancy. Art Deco developed between the World Wars and was based on geometric forms, using new materials and colour combinations to create a recognisable and popular style. San Sebastián is almost a temple to Art Nouveau, while cities all over Spain have many good examples of Deco, as do many other cities, particularly in old cinemas and theatres.

Modern architecture

Elegance and whimsy never seemed to play much part in fascist architecture, and during the Franco era Spain was subjected to an appalling series of ponderous concrete monoliths, all in the name of progress. A few avant-garde buildings managed to escape the drudgery from the 1950s on – the Basque monastery of Arantzazu is a spectacular example – but it was the dictator's death in 1975 followed by EEC membership in 1986 that really provided the impetus for change.

The Guggenheim Museum is the obvious example of the flowering that has taken place in the last few years in Spain, but it is only one of many. San Sebastián's Kursaal and Vitoria's shining Artium are both excellent examples of modern Spanish works, while the much-admired Valencian, Santiago Calatrava, has done much work for his home city and elsewhere. Zamora is also noteworthy as a city that has managed to combine sensitive modern design with the Romanesque heritage of its old town, while Sevilla and Barcelona have both benefited from hosting major world events (Expo and the Olympics in 1992) to give themselves a sleek 21st-century facelift. Much of Spain, however, is still plagued by the concrete curse on the outskirts of its major cities and in coastal areas, where lax planning laws are taken full and hideous advantage of.

Architectural traditions

Other architectural traditions worth mentioning are in Euskadi, where baserriak are large stone farmhouses with sloping roofs, built to last by the heads of families: many are very old. Their presence in the green Basque hills gives the place a distinctly non-Spanish air. The square wooded *horréos* of Asturias and their elongated stone counterparts in Galicia are trademarks of the region and have been used over the centuries as granaries and drying sheds, although those in Galicia are of a less practical design and were to some extent status symbols also. Cruceiros in Galicia are large stone crosses, most frequently carved with a scene of the Crucifixion. Mostly made from the 17th to the 19th centuries, they stand outside churches and along roads.

Art

Spain's artistic traditions go back a long way; right to the Palaeolithic, when cave artists along the north and southeast coasts produced art that ranged from simple outlines of hands to the beautiful and sophisticated bison herds of Altamira.

In the first millennium BC, Iberian and Celtic cultures produced fine jewellery from gold and silver, as well as some remarkable sculpture and ceramics. La Dama de Elche and La Dama de Baza are particularly fine busts that demonstrate significant influences from the eastern Mediterranean; they are to be found in Madrid's Museo Arqueológico. These influences derive from contact with trading posts set up by the Phoenicians, Greeks and Carthaginians; all three cultures have left artistic evidence of their presence, mostly in the port cities they established. Similarly, the Romans brought their own artistic styles to the peninsula, and there are many cultural remnants, mostly found in the south; these include a number of fine mosaïc floors.

Visigoths

Contrary to their wild and woolly reputation, the Visigoths were skilled artists and craftspeople, and produced many fine pieces, notably in metalwork. Madrid's archaeological museum holds an excellent ensemble found at their capital, Toledo, and there are some good items in the city itself. The finest examples of Visigothic art are delicately adorned gold and silver pieces commissioned by rulers; the style reflects the Germanic roots of the people.

Moors

The majority of the artistic heritage left by the Moors is tied up in their architecture. As Islamic law forbids the portrayal of human or animal figures, tradition favoured intricate decoration with calligraphic, geometric and vegetable themes predominating. Superb panelled ceilings are a feature of Almohad architecture; a particularly attractive style being that known as *artesonado*, in which the concave panels are bordered with elaborate inlay work. During this period, too, glazed tiles known as *azulejos* began to be produced; these continue to be a feature of Andalucían craftsmanship.

Meanwhile, free from Islamic artistic strictures, monks in the north produced some illustrated manuscripts of beauty in which their cloistered imaginations ran riot, particularly when dealing with creatures of the Apocalypse. Copies of the works of Beatus of Liébana are particularly outstanding and created from a tangible fear of a very real Hell.

Religious architecture

Away from the scriptoria, the outstanding examples of medieval Spanish art come from churches, where some superb fresco work has been preserved in situ, and in museums. Asturian pre-Romanesque buildings preserve some decoration, but the best examples are from Romanesque and Mozarabic churches. The Panteón (royal burial chamber) in the basílica of San Isidoro in León is stunning, as is the Mozarabic chapel of San Baudelio near Berlanga del Duero, although scandalously plundered by an American art dealer in the 1920s. Other particularly impressive ensembles from the period can be seen in the cathedral museum at Jaca in the Aragonese Pyrenees, and at the museum of Catalan art in Barcelona.

Romanesque

Romanesque art also hit lofty heights in the field of sculpture. Master masons responsible for such gems as the cloisters of San Juan de la Peña and Santo Domingo de Silos are not known by name, but achieved sculptural perfection, above all on the decorated capitals of the columns. Arguably the finest of them all is Master Mateo, whose tour de force was the Pórtico de la Gloria entrance to the cathedral at Santiago.

Other elements of Romanesque art that have come down to us include retablos (altarpieces or retables) and painted (the endearing jargon term 'polychrome' is more common) figures. These tend to be rendered in bright colours – as was the majority of stone sculpture, although wind and weather has usually stripped it off – and despite being fairly rigid and stylized by convention, many examples achieve significant beauty.

Gothic period

The Gothic style in Spain, like the Romanesque, arrived on more than one front. The Mediterranean coast, especially Valencia, was handily placed to receive architectural and artistic influences from Italy, while the north, boosted by the pilgrim traffic to Santiago, looked to France and northern Europe for its initial inspiration. Catalunya was in a position to pick and choose from both regions.

Over time, Gothic sculpture achieved more naturalism in rendering than in earlier periods. The style became more ornate too, culminating in the superlative technical mastery of the works of the northern Europeans resident in Castilla, Simón de Colonia, and Gil and Diego de Siloé, whose stunning retablos and tombs are mostly in and around Burgos. Damián Forment was a busy late Gothic sculptor who left his native Aragón to train in Italy, then returned and executed a fine series of retablos in his homeland. Saints and Virgins in polychrome wood continued popular, and there are some fine examples from the period.

As well as sculptors, there were many foreign painters working in the Gothic period in northern Spain. As well as retablos, painted panels on gold backgrounds were popular, often in the form of triptychs. Often depicting lives of saints, many of these are excellent pieces, combining well-rendered expression with a lively imagination, particularly when depicting demons, subjects where the artist had a freer rein. Some of the better painters from this period are Fernando Gallego, whose paintings grace Salamanca, Jorge Inglés, resident in Valladolid and presumably an Englishman named George, Juan de Flandes (Salamanca; Flanders), and Nicolás Francés (León; France). All these painters drew on influences from the Italian and Flemish schools of the time, but managed to create a distinctive and entertaining Spanish style.

Much of the finest Spanish Gothic art, however, came from the coastal portions of the kingdom of Aragón; Catalunya and Valencia, both of which gave their names to a school of Gothic painting. In the early 14th century, Ferrer Bassá was heavily influenced from Italy, particularly Siena. Notable later artists in these schools include Jaume Serra, Luis Borrassá, Pere Nicolau and Bernat Martorell, all of whom evolved towards a more Spanish style. Considered two of the greatest of the Gothic artists are Jaume Huguet and Bartolomé Bermejo, both of whom brought painting to new levels of realism, sensitivity and expression, the latter influenced by contemporary artists in Flanders.

Renaissance

The Renaissance in Spain, too, drew heavily on the Italian. The transitional painter Pedro Berruguete hailed from near Palencia and studied in Italy. His works are executed in the Gothic manner but have a Renaissance fluidity that was mastered by his son, Alonso, who learned under Michelangelo and was court painter to Carlos I (Charles V). His finest work is sculptural; he created saints of remarkable power and expression in marble and in wood. Juan de Juni lived in Valladolid and is also notable for his sensitive sculptures of religious themes.

The best-known 16th-century Spanish artist was actually born in Crete. After training in Italy, Domenikos Theotokopoulos got a commission in Toledo and stayed on because he liked the place. Known almost universally as El Greco ('the Greek'), he was a man somewhat ahead of his time. There's a haunted quality to much of his work, which uses misshapen faces and sombre colouring to create a sort of shadow-zone linking life and death. Some of his later works are almost surreal, while earlier in his career he was more conventionally Italian in style. His finest works are in Toledo and Madrid.

As the Renaissance progressed, naturalism in painting increased, leading into the 'Golden Age' of Spanish art. This was the finest period of Spanish painting; one of its early figures was the 16th-century Riojan painter Juan Fernández Navarrete, many of whose works are in the Escorial. He studied in Venice and his style earned him the nickname of the Spanish Titian; his paintings have a grace of expression denied him in speech by his dumbness.

Francisco Ribalta (1565-1628) learned tenebrism from his Italian contemporaries and brought it home with him to Spain; the majority of his work can be seen in his hometown of Valencia. His one-time pupil, José de Ribera (1591-1652), resident in the Spanish territory of Naples, also took plenty of Italian techniques on board. One of the foremost European painters of his day, he had a huge influence on those who came after, such as Velásquez and Murillo. He was prolific, but rarely compromised his style, which often depicted fairly gruesome martyrdoms and the like with powerful characterization of the main protagonists.

As Sevilla prospered on New World riches, the city became a centre for artists, who found wealthy patrons in abundance. Pre-eminent among all was Diego Rodríguez de Silva Velásquez (1599-1660), who started his career there before moving to Madrid to become a court painter. A consummate portraitist, he was far more a realist than any of his predecessors, and in some cases seems almost to have captured the subject's soul on canvas, such as in his depictions of the haunted Habsburg Philip IV. His most famous work, Las Meninas, depicts the young princess Margarita surrounded by courtiers, including a dwarf, always favourite companions for the Habsburgs. The artist himself appears, brush in hand, as does a reflection of the watching king. The perspective puzzles that Velásquez poses, as well as the sheer mastery of execution, make this one of the most remarkable of paintings.

Another remarkable painter working in Sevilla was Francisco de Zurbarán (1598-1664). While he produced plenty of high-speed dross on commission, his best works are from the topmost drawer of European art. His idiosyncratic style often focuses on superbly rendered white garments in a dark, brooding background, a metaphor for the subjects themselves, who were frequently priests. His paintings can be seen throughout Spain, above all in Andalucía. His Crucifixions are particularly memorable, full of despair and anguish, even if, as in one Prado example, his patrons sometimes chose to appear in the painting at Christ's feet; perhaps so that at dinner parties they could tell their friends that they'd been there…

During Zurbarán's later years, he was eclipsed in the Sevilla popularity stakes by Bartolomé Esteban Murillo (1618-1682). While at first glance his paintings can seem somewhat heavy on the sentimentality, they tend to focus on the space between the central characters, who interact with glances or gestures of great power and meaning. The religious atmosphere of imperial Spain continued to dominate in art; landscapes and joie de vivre are in comparatively short supply. Juan Valdés Leal certainly had little of the latter; his macabre realist paintings include a famous Sevilla example, Finis Gloriae Mundi, which shows a dead bishop being devoured by worms.

A fine portraitist overshadowed by his contemporary Velásquez was the Asturian noble Juan Carreño de Miranda (1614-1685). Late in life he became court painter and is noted for his depictions of the unfortunate inbreed king Carlos II. Of the so-called 'Madrid school', the most worthwhile painter is Claudio Coello, who painted portraits for the court as well as larger figured tableaux; some of his works hang in the Escorial.

Gregorio Hernández was a fine naturalistic sculptor working in Valladolid at this time, while in Andalucía Juan Martínez Montañés carved numerous figures, retablos, and pasos (ornamental floats for religious processions) in wood. Alonso Cano was a talented painter and sculptor working from Granada. The main focus of this medium continued to be ecclesiastic; retablos became ever larger and more ornate, commissioned by nobles to gain favour with the church and improve their chances in the afterlife. As the Baroque period progressed, this was taken to ridiculous degree. Some of the altarpieces and canopies are immense and overgilded, clashing horribly with the sober Gothic lines of the churches they were placed in; while supremely competent in execution, they can seem gaudy and ostentatious to modern eyes.

Bourbon Art

The early 18th century saw fairly characterless art produced under the new dynasty of Bourbon kings. Tapestry production increased markedly but never scaled the heights of the earlier Flemish masterpieces, many of which can be seen in northern Spain. The appropriately-enough named Francisco Bayeu produced pictures for tapestries ('cartoons'), as did the master of 19th-century art, Francisco Goya.

Goya was a remarkable figure whose finest works included both paintings and etchings; his fresco work in northern Spanish churches never scaled these heights. His depiction of the vain Bourbon royals is brutally accurate; he was no fan of the royal family, and as court painter got away with murder. His etchings of the horrors of the Napoleonic wars are another facet of his uncompromising depictions. His nightmarish 'black paintings', painted on the walls of his cottage as an old man in a state of semi-dementia, are an unforgettable highlight of Madrid's Prado.

Generation of 1898

After Goya, the 19th century produced few works of note as Spain tore itself apart in a series of brutal wars and conflicts. The rebirth came at the end of the period with the '1898 generation' (see Literature below). One of their number was the Basque painter Ignacio Zuloaga (1870-1945), a likeable artist with a love of Spain and a clear eye for its tragic aspects. His best work is portraiture, often set against a brooding Castillian landscape. His contemporary, Joaquín Sorolla (1863-1923), is best known for his depictions of his native Valencian beaches, which enjoyably reflect the Spain in which he lived.

Modernism and surrealism

The early 20th century saw the rise of Spanish modernism and surrealism, much of it driven from Catalunya. While architects such as Gaudí managed to combine their discipline with art, it was one man from Málaga who had such an influence on 20th century painting that he is arguably the most famous artist in the world. Pablo Ruíz Picasso (1881-1973) is notable not just for his artistic genius, but also for his evolution through different styles. Training in Barcelona, but doing much of his work in Paris, his initial Blue Period was fairly sober and subdued, named for predominant use of that colour. His best early work, however, came in his succeeding 'Pink Period', where he used brighter tones to depict the French capital. He moved on from this to become a pioneer of cubism. Drawing on non-western forms, cubism forsook realism for a new form of three-dimensionality, trying to show subjects from as many different angles as possible. Picasso then moved on to more surrealist forms. He continued painting right throughout his lifetime and produced an incredible number of works. One of his best-known paintings is Guernica, a nightmarish ensemble of terror-struck animals and people that he produced in abhorrence at the Nationalist bombing of the defenceless Basque market town in April 1937. Juan Gris was another Spanish cubist whose fluid compositions are widely seen across European galleries.

While Catalonians tend to claim Picasso due to the Barcelona connection, the region produced two of the greats of 20th century art in its own right; Joan Miró and Salvador Dalí. Dalí (1904-1989) goes under the label of surrealism often enough, but in reality his style was completely his own. His best paintings are visions of his own dreamworlds, spaces filled with unlikely objects and strange perspectives, but created with the most precise of brushwork. Miró (1893-1983) was a cheerier type, a fan of bright colours and bold lines, the sort of bloke (Joan is the Catalan version of Juan) that grumblers complain 'my kid could do better' about.

The Civil War was to have a serious effect, as a majority of artists sided with the Republic and fled Spain with their defeat. Franco was far from an enlightened patron of the arts, and his occupancy was a monotonous time. One of the main lights in this period came from the Basque lands in the 1950s. Painters such as Nestor Barretxea, and the sculptors Eduardo Chillida and Jorge Oteiza were part of a revival; all three are represented at the tradition-defying monastery of Arantzazu. Chillida (who died in 2002) and Oteiza have continued to be at the forefront of modern sculpture, and their works are widespread through Northern Spain and Europe. Other sculptors such as the Zaragozans Pablo Serrano and Pablo Gargallo are also prominent.

The 1950s also saw the rise of the Generación Abstracta, a single movement who based themselves in Cuenca. The overtly political Antonio Saura is the best of these; his large black and white compositions are unmistakeable. Antoní Tàpies experimented with a wide range of materials.

The provincial governments of Spain are extremely supportive of local artists these days, and the museums in each provincial capital usually have a good collection of modern works, among which female artists are finally being adequately represented; even more than in other nations, the history of Spanish art is a male one.

Contents

122 Useful words and phrases

125 Food glosary

126 Index

Footnotes

Useful words and phrases

Spanish words and phrases

Greetings, courtesies

hello	*hola*	thank you (very much)	*(muchas) gracias*
good morning	*buenos días*	I speak Spanish	*hablo español*
good afternoon/evening	*buenas tardes/noches*	I don't speak Spanish	*no hablo español*
		do you speak English?	*¿habla inglés?*
goodbye	*adiós/chao*	I don't understand	*no entiendo/no comprendo*
pleased to meet you	*mucho gusto*		
how are you?	*¿cómo está?*	please speak slowly	*hable despacio por favor*
	¿cómo estás?		
I'm fine, thanks	*estoy muy bien, gracias*	I am very sorry	*lo siento mucho/disculpe*
I'm called...	*me llamo ...*	what do you want?	*¿qué quiere?*
what is your name?	*¿cómo se llama?*		*¿qué quieres?*
	¿cómo te llamas?	I want/would like	*quiero/quería*
yes/no	*sí/no*	I don't want it	*no lo quiero*
please	*por favor*	good/bad	*bueno/malo*

Basic questions and requests

have you got a room for two people?	*¿tiene una habitación para dos personas?*
how do I get to_?	*¿cómo llego a_?*
how much does it cost?	*¿cuánto vale? ¿cuánto es?*
is service included?	*¿está incluido el servicio?*
is tax included?	*¿están incluidos los impuestos?*
when does the bus leave (arrive)?	*¿a qué hora sale (llega) el autobús?*
when?	*¿cuándo?*
where is_?	*¿dónde está_?*
where can I buy tickets?	*¿dónde puedo comprar boletos?*
where is the nearest gas station?	*¿dónde está la gasolinera más cercana?*
why?	*¿por qué?*

Basic words and phrases

bank	*el banco*	exchange rate	*el tipo de cambio*
bathroom/toilet	*el baño*	expensive	*caro/a*
to be	*ser, estar*	to go	*ir*
bill	*la cuenta*	to have	*tener, haber*
cash	*el efectivo*	market	*el mercado*
cheap	*barato/a*	note/coin	*el billete/la moneda*
credit card	*la tarjeta de crédito*	police (policeman)	*la policía (el policía)*
exchange house	*la casa de cambio*	post office	*el correo*

public telephone	el teléfono público	there isn't/aren't	no hay
shop	la tienda	ticket office	la taquilla
supermarket	el supermercado	traveller's cheques	los cheques de viajero
there is/are	hay		

Getting around

aeroplane	el avión	luggage	el equipaje
airport	el aeropuerto	motorway, freeway	el autopista/autovía
arrival/departure	la llegada/salida	north, south	el norte, el sur
avenue	la avenida	west, east	el oeste , el este
border	la frontera	oil	el aceite
bus station	la estación de autobuses	to park	aparcar
bus	el bus/el autobús/	passport	el pasaporte
	el camión	petrol/gasoline	la gasolina
corner	la esquina	puncture	el pinchazo
customs	la aduana	street	la calle
left/right	izquierda/derecha	that way	por allí
ticket	el billete	this way	por aquí
empty/full	vacío/lleno	tyre	el neumático
highway, main road	la carretera	waiting room	la sala de espera
insurance	el seguro	to walk	caminar/andar
insured person	el asegurado/la asegurada		

Accommodation

air conditioning	el aire acondicionado	pillow	la almohada
all-inclusive	todo incluido	restaurant	el restaurante
bathroom, private	el baño privado	room/bedroom	el cuarto/la habitación
bed, double/single	la cama	sheets	las sábanas
	matrimonial/sencilla	shower	la ducha
blankets	las mantas	soap	el jabón
to clean	limpiar	toilet	el inodoro
dining room	el comedor	toilet paper	el papel higiénico
hotel	el hotel	towels, clean/dirty	las toallas limpias/sucias
noisy	ruidoso	water, hot/cold	el agua caliente/fría

Health

aspirin	la aspirina	diarrhoea	la diarrea
blood	la sangre	doctor	el médico
chemist	la farmacia	fever/sweat	la fiebre/el sudor
condoms	los preservativos,	pain	el dolor
	los condones	head	la cabeza
contact lenses	los lentes de contacto	period/sanitary towels	la regla/las toallas
contraceptives	los anticonceptivos		femininas
contraceptive pill	la píldora	stomach	el estómago
	anticonceptiva		

Family

family	*la familia*		*la mujer*
brother/sister	*el hermano/ la hermana*	boyfriend/girlfriend	*el novio/la novia*
		friend	*el amigo/la amiga*
daughter/son	*la hija/el hijo*	married	*casado/a*
father/mother	*el padre/la madre*	single/unmarried	*soltero/a*
husband/wife	*el esposo (marido)/*		

Months, days and time

January	*enero*	July	*julio*
February	*febrero*	August	*agosto*
March	*marzo*	September	*septiembre*
April	*abril*	October	*octubre*
May	*mayo*	November	*noviembre*
June	*junio*	December	*diciembre*

Monday	*lunes*	Friday	*viernes*
Tuesday	*martes*	Saturday	*sábado*
Wednesday	*miércoles*	Sunday	*domingo*
Thursday	*jueves*		

at one o'clock	*a la una*	it's six twenty	*son las seis y veinte*
at half past two	*a las dos y media*	it's five to nine	*son las nueve menos cinco*
at a quarter to three	*a las tres menos cuarto*	in ten minutes	*en diez minutos*
		five hours	*cinco horas*
it's one o'clock	*es la una*	does it take long?	*¿tarda mucho?*
it's seven o'clock	*son las siete*		

Numbers

one	*uno*	sixteen	*dieciséis*
two	*dos*	seventeen	*diecisiete*
three	*tres*	eighteen	*dieciocho*
four	*cuatro*	nineteen	*diecinueve*
five	*cinco*	twenty	*veinte*
six	*seis*	twenty-one	*veintiuno*
seven	*siete*	thirty	*treinta*
eight	*ocho*	forty	*cuarenta*
nine	*nueve*	fifty	*cincuenta*
ten	*diez*	sixty	*sesenta*
eleven	*once*	seventy	*setenta*
twelve	*doce*	eighty	*ochenta*
thirteen	*trece*	ninety	*noventa*
fourteen	*catorce*	hundred	*cien/ciento*
fifteen	*quince*	thousand	*mil*

Food glossary → *See also Food and drink, page 12.*

It is impossible to be definitive about terms used. Different regions have numerous variants.

agua water
ahumado smoked
ajo garlic; *ajillo* means cooked in garlic, most commonly *gambas* or *pollo*
albóndigas meatballs
alcaparras capers
almejas small clams
alubias beans
anchoa preserved anchovy
atun tuna
bacalao salted cod
berenjena aubergine/eggplant
bistek steak
boquerones fresh anchovies
caballa mackerel
cabrito young goat, usually roasted
calamares squid
caldereta a stew of meat or fish
caldo a thin soup
callo tripe
carne meat
cazuela a stew, often of fish or seafood
cerdo pork
chipirones small squid
choco cuttlefish
chorizo a cured red sausage
chuleta/chuletilla chop
chuletón a massive T-bone steak
churro a fried dough-stick usually eaten with hot chocolate (*chocolate con churros*).
cigala giant prawn
cochinillo/lechón/tostón suckling pig
cocido a heavy stew, usually of meat and chickpeas/beans; *sopa de cocido* is the broth
cordero lamb
embutido any salami-type sausage
empanada a savoury pie
gambas prawns
higado liver
jamón ham
leche milk

lechuga lettuce
lenguado sole
lentejas lentils
lomo loin, usually sliced pork
lubina sea bass
Manchego Spain's national cheese made from ewe's milk
mantequilla butter
manzana apple
marisco shellfish
mejillones mussels
menudo tripe stew
merluza hake
mero grouper
miel honey
morcilla blood sausage
navajas razor-shells
ostra oyster
parrilla a mixed grill
pato duck
pechuga breast (usually chicken)
percebes goose-neck barnacles
pescado fish
pimientos peppers
pintxo/pincho bartop snack
pipas sunflower seeds, a common snack
pollo chicken
pulpo octopus
queso cheese
rape monkfish
relleno/a stuffed
revuelto scrambled eggs
riñones kidneys
salchichón a salami-like sausage
salmorejo a thicker version of *gazpacho*,
salpicón a seafood salad
secreto a cut of pork loin
sepia cuttlefish
setas wild mushrooms, often superb
solomillo beef fillet steak
zanahoria carrot

Index

A

accommodation 10
  price codes 11
activities 71
agroturismos 11
air 6
airport information 6
albergues 11
Alcalá de Henares 88
Aranjuez 89
architecture 108
Arenas de San Pedro 87
art 115
Ateneo Artístico, Científico y
  Literario de Madrid 38
Atocha 47
Ávila 82

B

banks 73
bars and clubs 64
Basilica de San Francisco el
  Grande 50
beer 17
Biblioteca Nacional 56
Buitrago de Lozoya 77
bus 8

C

cafés 18
CaixaForum 46
Calle Alcalá 51
Calle Arenal 34
Calle Atocha 39
Calle Huertas 39
Camera de Son Jeronimo 39
camping 12
car 7
car hire 9
Casa de América 55
Casa de Campo 54
Casa de la Villa 34
Casa-Museo de El Greco 95
Casa Museo Lope de Vega 39
Casón del Buen Retiro 45
Castellano 21

Catedral de Nuestra Señora de la
  Almudena 37
Catedral de San Isidro 49
Centro Cultural Conde Duque 54
Cepada y Ahumada, de Teresa
  83
Cercedilla 76
Chillida, Eduardo 120
Chinchón 90
Chueca 52
cider 17
Cine Dore 39
cinema 67
climate 6
coach 7
Congreso de los Diputados 40
consulates 21
Convento de la Encarnación 37
Convento de Santa Teresa, Ávila
  85
Corpus Christi 104
Cortes 39
cost of living 22
Cotos 77
crime 23
currency 21
cycling 9

D

Dalí, Salvador 119
dance 67
directory 73
drinks 16

E

El Barco de Ávila 87
El Dos de Mayo 54
El Escorial 75
El Greco 94
El Rastro 50
electricity 21
embassies 21
emergencies 21
entertainment 66
Ermita de San Antonio de la
  Florida 54
Estación Atocha 47

F

Fábrica de Tabacos 50
ferry 7
festivals 10
fiestas 19
  Madrid 69
fish 12
flamenco 67
flights 6
food 12
  food glossary 125
football 45
  Madrid 68
Fundación Juan March 57

G

Goya, Francisco 119
Gran Vía 51

H

health 21
hospitals 21
  Madrid 73
hotels 10
  Madrid 58
Hoyos del Espino 87

I

immigration 24
insurance 21

L

La Granja de San Ildefonso 81
La Latina 48
language 21
  useful words and phrases 122
language schools 72
La Residencia de Estudiantes 57
Lavapiés 50

M

Madrid 26-73
  airport 6
  listings 73
  places in Madrid 30
  transport 72

Malasaña 53
Manzanares La Real 77
maps 10
markets 71
Mercado de San Miguel 34
Miró, Joan 119
mobile phones 23
Modernista 114
Monasterio de las Descalzas
    Reales 35
money 21
motorcycling 10
Mudéjar 112
Muralla de Ávila 83
Museo Antropología 48
Museo Arqueológico 56
Museo Cerralbo 52
Museo de América 54
Museo de San Isidro 48
Museo del Ejército 45
Museo del Ferrocarril 47
Museo del Prado 41
Museo Historia de Madrid 52
Museo Lázaro Galdiano 56
Museo Municipal 52
Museo Nacional Centro de Arte
    de Reina Sofla 44
Museo Nacional des Artes
    Decoratives 46
Museo Naval 46
Museo Pantéon de Goya 53
Museo del Romanticismo 53
Museo Sorolla 56
Museo Thyssen-Bornemisza 43
music 68

N
Navacerrada 77
Navarredonda de Gredos 87
nightclubs 64
Nuevo Báztan 89

O
Oteiza, Jorge 120

P
palace gardens 37
Palacio de Linares 55
Palacio Marqués de Salamanca 55
Palacio Real 36
Panteón des Hombres Ilustres 48

paradors 11
Parque del Oeste 54
Parque del Retiro 46
Paseo de la Castellana 56
Paseo de Recoletas 55
Paseo del Prado 45
pensiones 10
Picasso, Pablo 119
Piedrahlta 87
Plaza de Chueca 52
Plaza de Dos de Mayo 53
Plaza de España 52
Plaza de la Armeria 37
Plaza de la Lealtad 51
Plaza de la Paja 48
Plaza de la Villa 34
Plaza de Oriente 35
Plaza de Santa Ana 38
Plaza del Callao 52
Plaza Mayor 31
Prado 40
Puerta de Toledo 50
Puerta del Sol 31
public holidays 20

R
rail travel, see train
Rastro 50
Real Academia de Bellas Artes de
    San Fernando 51
Real Fábrica de Tapices 48
Real Jardin Botánico 46
Real Monasterio de San Lorenzo
    el Real de El Escorial 75
refugios 11
RENFE 8
restaurant price codes 11
restaurants 18
Ríofrío 82
rural homes 11

S
safety 23
Salamanca 55
San Isidro festival 69
seafood 12
Segovia 77
shopping 70
Sierra de Gredos 86
Sierra de Guadarrama 75-76
Sociedad General de Autores 53
Spanish 21
surrealism 119

T
tax 22
taxi 10
Teatro Español 38
Teatro Real 36
téléferico 54
telephone 23
Teresa de Cepada y Ahumada 83
theatre 68
time zones 24
tipping 24
toilets 24
Toledo 91
Torre de los Lujanes 35
Torre Telefónica 51
tortilla 15
tourist offices 24
    Madrid 30
tours 71
train 6, 8
transport 6
    air 6
    boat 7
    bus 8
    car 7-8
    coach 7
    cycling 9
    motorcycling 10
    rail 6, 8
    sea 7
    taxis 10
    train 6
Triangulo del Arte 40

V
Valle de los Calídos 76
Valley of the Fallen 76
Vega, de Lope 38
vegetarian food 19
Ventas 57
visas 24

W
weather 6
wine 16

Z
Zurbarán 118

Titles available in the Footprint *Focus* range

Latin America	UK RRP	US RRP
Bahia & Salvador	£7.99	$11.95
Brazilian Amazon	£7.99	$11.95
Brazilian Pantanal	£6.99	$9.95
Buenos Aires & Pampas	£7.99	$11.95
Cartagena & Caribbean Coast	£7.99	$11.95
Costa Rica	£8.99	$12.95
Cuzco, La Paz & Lake Titicaca	£8.99	$12.95
El Salvador	£5.99	$8.95
Guadalajara & Pacific Coast	£6.99	$9.95
Guatemala	£8.99	$12.95
Guyana, Guyane & Suriname	£5.99	$8.95
Havana	£6.99	$9.95
Honduras	£7.99	$11.95
Nicaragua	£7.99	$11.95
Northeast Argentina & Uruguay	£8.99	$12.95
Paraguay	£5.99	$8.95
Quito & Galápagos Islands	£7.99	$11.95
Recife & Northeast Brazil	£7.99	$11.95
Rio de Janeiro	£8.99	$12.95
São Paulo	£5.99	$8.95
Uruguay	£6.99	$9.95
Venezuela	£8.99	$12.95
Yucatán Peninsula	£6.99	$9.95

Asia	UK RRP	US RRP
Angkor Wat	£5.99	$8.95
Bali & Lombok	£8.99	$12.95
Chennai & Tamil Nadu	£8.99	$12.95
Chiang Mai & Northern Thailand	£7.99	$11.95
Goa	£6.99	$9.95
Gulf of Thailand	£8.99	$12.95
Hanoi & Northern Vietnam	£8.99	$12.95
Ho Chi Minh City & Mekong Delta	£7.99	$11.95
Java	£7.99	$11.95
Kerala	£7.99	$11.95
Kolkata & West Bengal	£5.99	$8.95
Mumbai & Gujarat	£8.99	$12.95

Africa & Middle East	UK RRP	US RRP
Beirut	£6.99	$9.95
Cairo & Nile Delta	£8.99	$12.95
Damascus	£5.99	$8.95
Durban & KwaZulu Natal	£8.99	$12.95
Fès & Northern Morocco	£8.99	$12.95
Jerusalem	£8.99	$12.95
Johannesburg & Kruger National Park	£7.99	$11.95
Kenya's Beaches	£8.99	$12.95
Kilimanjaro & Northern Tanzania	£8.99	$12.95
Luxor to Aswan	£8.99	$12.95
Nairobi & Rift Valley	£7.99	$11.95
Red Sea & Sinai	£7.99	$11.95
Zanzibar & Pemba	£7.99	$11.95

Europe	UK RRP	US RRP
Bilbao & Basque Region	£6.99	$9.95
Brittany West Coast	£7.99	$11.95
Cádiz & Costa de la Luz	£6.99	$9.95
Granada & Sierra Nevada	£6.99	$9.95
Languedoc: Carcassonne to Montpellier	£7.99	$11.95
Málaga	£5.99	$8.95
Marseille & Western Provence	£7.99	$11.95
Orkney & Shetland Islands	£5.99	$8.95
Santander & Picos de Europa	£7.99	$11.95
Sardinia: Alghero & the North	£7.99	$11.95
Sardinia: Cagliari & the South	£7.99	$11.95
Seville	£5.99	$8.95
Sicily: Palermo & the Northwest	£7.99	$11.95
Sicily: Catania & the Southeast	£7.99	$11.95
Siena & Southern Tuscany	£7.99	$11.95
Sorrento, Capri & Amalfi Coast	£6.99	$9.95
Skye & Outer Hebrides	£6.99	$9.95
Verona & Lake Garda	£7.99	$11.95

North America	UK RRP	US RRP
Vancouver & Rockies	£8.99	$12.95

Australasia	UK RRP	US RRP
Brisbane & Queensland	£8.99	$12.95
Perth	£7.99	$11.95

For the latest books, e-books and a wealth of travel information, visit us at:
www.footprinttravelguides.com.

footprinttravelguides.com

Join us on facebook for the latest travel news, product releases, offers and amazing competitions:
www.facebook.com/footprintbooks.